Into the Universe of Technical Images

Electronic Mediations

Katherine Hayles, Mark Poster,
and Samuel Weber, Series Editors

(continued on page 194)

Into the Universe of Technical Images

Vilém Flusser

Introduction by Mark Poster
Translated by Nancy Ann Roth

Electronic Mediations
VOLUME 32

 University of Minnesota Press
MINNEAPOLIS · LONDON

Originally published as *Ins Universum der technischen Bilder.*
Copyright 1985 European Photography, Andreas Müller-
Pohle, P. O. Box 08 02 27, D-10002 Berlin, Germany, www.
equivalence.com. Edition Flusser, Volume IV (2000[6]).

Published by the University of Minnesota Press
111 Third Avenue South, Suite 290
Minneapolis, MN 55401–2520
http://www.upress.umn.edu

Library of Congress Cataloging-in-Publication Data

Flusser, Vilém, 1920–1991.
  [Ins Universum der technischen Bilder. English]
  Into the universe of technical images / Vilém Flusser ;
introduction by Mark Poster ; translated by Nancy Ann Roth.
    p. cm. — (Electronic mediations ; v. 32)
  Includes bibliographical references and index.
  ISBN 978-0-8166-7020-8 (hc : alk. paper)
  ISBN 978-0-8166-7021-5 (pb : alk. paper)
1. Photography—Philosophy. I. Title.
  TR183.F5813 2011
  770.1—dc22
                    2010030720

Printed in the United States of America on acid-free paper

The University of Minnesota is an equal-opportunity educator
and employer.

17 16 15 14 13 12 11   10 9 8 7 6 5 4 3 2 1

Without Andreas Müller-Pohle, whose photographic and theoretical work has had a strong influence on me, this book would either not have been written at all or would have been written very differently.

—V. F.

Contents

Into the Universe of Technical Images

An Introduction to Vilém Flusser's *Into the Universe of Technical Images* and *Does Writing Have a Future?*

Mark Poster

Vilém Flusser remains relatively unknown to readers of critical theory, cultural studies, and media studies, particularly among readers of English. Given this, the Electronic Mediations series of the University of Minnesota Press herewith publishes in English translation two of his most important works, *Does Writing Have a Future?* and *Into the Universe of Technical Images,* both translated by Nancy Ann Roth. We trust that these publications, in addition to those already available from this and other presses, will bring Flusser's ideas to a wider English audience. Flusser ought not to require an introduction such as I provide because his work is crucial to a world saturated by a culture highly dependent on media. The production, reproduction, consumption, dissemination, and storage of texts, images, and sounds increasingly rely on electronic devices, almost always nowadays in a digital format. The immense implication of the dramatic spread of media in everyday life is beginning to dawn on most of us. Yet much remains to be done in theorizing information media and studying it empirically.

Many obstacles stand in the way of fresh thinking about media. Media are surely central to Western societies of the past several centuries and to the emerging global societies of the contemporary era and the future. There is a thickening, intensification, and increasing complexity to the use of information machines, technologies that are necessary in the production, reproduction, storage, and distribution of texts, images, and sounds—the constituent elements of culture. This phenomenon has been termed a "media ecology,"[1] adding a new layer to the ecologies of animal, vegetable, and mineral. It behooves anyone engaged in critical discourse to take serious account of media. I argue that media offer a key to understanding the process of globalization in relation to a new configuration of interaction between humans and machines.

Media are not easy to define, and one's approach to them affects considerably the character and limits of one's discourse. All too often, media are generalized and made transcendent, as in the characteristic gesture of Western theory in which humans are tool-making animals, enjoying the benefits of their tools "for the relief of man's estate," as Francis Bacon put it a half millennium ago.[2] Descartes provided the metaphysics to Bacon's utopian imaginings: humans are spirit, subjects for whom material workings, including of the human body, comprise little more than inert matter to be shaped and fashioned for human betterment. This ontology oscillates between praising the freedom of the human mind and cringing with anxiety at the possibility of its diminution should these external objects rise up and threaten it. The name for this threat is *technological determinism,* so poignantly portrayed by Charlie Chaplin in the film *Modern Times.*

Another problematic aspect of the Western figure of the tool-making animal is the confounding of media with technology. Machines that process texts, images, and sounds, I contend, are significantly distinct from machines that act on materials like wood and iron. However important these mechanical machines are, they are very different and have very different implications from information machines. Media machines act on the components of culture, not nature (if that distinction may still be employed), affecting human beings in a way very different from mechanical machines. One might say that information machines are closer to humans than mechanical machines and establish relations with them that are more profound.

It is urgent to rid critical discourse of the older framework of tool-making creatures and seek openings to the comprehension of the relation of humans to information machines, openings that promise alternatives to the binary of freedom and determinism. Such frameworks would need to acknowledge the logics of both the human and the machine as well as the logics of their various and multiple interactions. They would account for the interface between the two as well as the extension of their interactions across the planet, often violating political and cultural boundaries and forming new domains of politics and culture. These are the weighty issues raised by the simple term *media*. One theorist who braved these paths was Vilém Flusser.

Vilém Flusser can be compared to Marshall McLuhan and Jean Baudrillard. Similar to McLuhan, Flusser takes media seriously, and as does Baudrillard, he discerns the impact of media on culture. Like both McLuhan and Baudrillard, Flusser theorized media culture well before many other cultural theorists thought seriously about it. (There are certainly some notable exceptions: Walter Benjamin, Harold Innis, and Hans Magnus Enzensberger come immediately to mind.) Michel Foucault, Jacques Lacan, Louis Althusser, Jean-François Lyotard, Jürgen Habermas, Ernesto Laclau, Homi K. Bhabha, and Judith Butler—the list could be extended considerably of major theorists from the 1970s onward who either paid no attention at all to the vast changes in media culture taking place under their noses or who commented on the media only as a tool that amplified other institutions like capitalism or representative democracy. Against this group of thinkers, Flusser stands out, with only a handful of others, as one who presciently and insightfully deciphered the codes of materiality disseminated under the apparatuses of the media.

Perhaps one reason for the relative lack of attention to media by cultural theorists was the polemical antics of McLuhan, Baudrillard, and Flusser. The Canadian, the Frenchman, and the Czech all reveled in poking fun at those who failed to see the importance of media. Like McLuhan, Flusser repeatedly hailed the end of print and the onset of the age of images. He opens his book on writing, for example, with the following: "Writing, in the sense of placing letters and other marks one after another, appears to have little or no future."[3] Just as McLuhan pronounced the end of the "Gutenberg Galaxy," so Flusser proclaimed the end of writing. Neither would appeal much to a theoretical world that was discovering the importance of language, writing, and so forth. And in a mental habitus of scorn for popular culture, all three took seriously the importance of television (McLuhan), style (Baudrillard), and popularizing and extending symbolic exchanges on the global network (Flusser). One might say the importance of their work rests not so much with their insight into the phenomena of electronic media but with the simple and more basic fact that they paid attention to it at all.

Characteristic criticism of Flusser is found in an essay by Friedrich Kittler. Kittler objects to the sharp distinction drawn by McLuhan and Flusser between print and images:

> Media theorists, specifically Marshall McLuhan and, succeeding him, Vilem Flusser, draw an absolute distinction between writing and the image that ultimately rests on concepts of geometry. They contrast the linearity or one-dimensionality of printed books with the irreducible two-dimensionality of images. Simplified in this manner, it is a distinction that may hold true even when computer technology can model texts as strings, as it does today. But it suppresses the simple facts emphasized long ago and, not coincidentally, by a *nouveau romancier,* Michel Butor: the books used most often—the Bible, once upon a time, and today more likely the telephone book—are certainly not read in a linear manner.[4]

Kittler's critique of the binary print–image serves a cautionary role against overgeneralization but does not grapple with the basic issue of media specificity and its cultural implications. His critique is somewhat puzzling given his Foucauldian, historical approach to media, in which "discourse networks" are defined by epochs and are accordingly decidedly different from one another.[5]

One area of Flusser's media theory that deserves special attention is the connection he drew between writing and history and the implications of this analysis for a concept of temporality. In his discussions of media and history, Flusser—one might say without exaggeration—denaturalizes temporality with a systematicity not seen perhaps since Vico.[6] Flusser first argues that history is not possible without writing:

> With the invention of writing, history begins, not because writing keeps a firm hold on processes, but because it transforms scenes into processes: it generates historical consciousness.[7]

In the relation Flusser draws between writing and history, media practice already plays a central role in culture, in this case, as the awareness of time as linear movement. But already for him, "writing" performs the function of changing "scenes into processes." Thereby Flusser contrasts culture based on writing with culture based on images. In contrast to Derrida, Flusser associates the institution of writing not so much with a change in the form of memory (as *différance*) but with resistance to images: "Greek philosophy and Jewish prophecy are battle cries against images on behalf of texts."[8] Whereas for Derrida, the ancient Greeks at least focused on the danger of writing in comparison to speech, Flusser's binary of writing and images yields a different conclusion regarding the Greek valuation of writing.

What becomes most salient for Flusser's theory of media is the consequence of writing for temporality. Flusser makes a great deal

of the fact that writing is linear—that in this medium, one thing
inexorably comes after another. One cannot easily skip around in
a written text (i.e., until hypertext emerged with the digitization
of writing). Try as they might, theorists such as Roland Barthes
and writers from Laurence Sterne to Raymond Quéneau and the
Oulipo group have at best great difficulty in constructing texts that
allow or encourage the reader to find her own way through the
page.[9] Flusser's insistence on the linearity of writing, despite these
exceptions and demurrals, is convincing. He writes,

> Linear codes demand a synchronization of their diachronic-
> ity. They demand progressive reception. And the result is
> a new experience of time, that is, linear time, a stream of
> unstoppable progress, of dramatic unrepeatability, of fram-
> ing, in short, history.[10]

It might be noted that for the most part, historians have tra-
ditionally sided with Flusser on the question of the relation of
history to writing but not usually for the same reasons. Historians
claim that without writing, there is no material, objective basis for
memory about the past; as Flusser says, writing keeps "a firm hold
on the past." Put differently, Flusser distinguishes his argument
regarding the relation of writing to history from the argument of
historians as follows:

> The difference between prehistory and history is not that we
> have written documents . . . , but that during history there
> are literate men who experience, understand, and evaluate
> the world as a "becoming."[11]

Societies without writing are thereby societies without history.
Historians' penchant for the fullness of the written text, and the
face value of truth contained therein, is, of course, not Flusser's
claim. Not perhaps until the second half of the twentieth century,

with studies of the Holocaust[12] and other traumatic experiences more generally, have historians reconsidered the unique value of writing for their discipline, opening up the possibility that historical research might find evidentiary truth in oral reports and by conducting interviews. Also, influenced by anthropological and archeological methods, some historians consider material artifacts, objects without writing, at least as a supplementary source for their archives.

But Flusser's argument for the relation of writing to temporality has not been a major focus of historians. Flusser stresses the unidirectional flow of writing as well as its "unrepeatability" as prominent aspects of this medium, aspects that militate, if not determine, a cultural inscription of time as progressive. For Flusser, practices of writing and reading induce a linear sense of time and give prominence to diachronicity in general as compared with synchronicity. For Flusser, modern society's break with the general human sense of time as cyclical, an obvious extrapolation from nature's rhythms, owes a deep debt to the increasing salience of writing over the past several centuries. The full extension of time as a linear progression emerged not with the simple discovery of writing but with a number of social and cultural changes commensurate with modern society: the printing press that made writing widely reproducible, the spread of compulsory education in modern democracies, the rise of urban commercial cultures with their heavy reliance on written documents, the emergence of the modern state with its bureaucratic form, and so forth.

There is another facet to Flusser's theory of writing and temporality that deserves mention. For Flusser, writing as a medium encourages a specific form of temporality. The medium and the character of time are particular. This suggests that each medium might have an associated, special form of temporality. Flusser's media theory thereby accounts for the specificity of each information technology. His view contrasts sharply with Derrida's view in the sense that the latter understands the temporal logic of writing as paradigmatic for all media—indeed, for all technology. As a result, deconstruction has difficulty distinguishing between media cultures such as between writing cultures and image cultures. Bernard Stiegler finds fault with Derrida on precisely these grounds,[13] with the consequence that the relation of media technology to time is very different in the views of Derrida and Flusser.

If history, for Flusser, is a linear mode of consciousness related to writing, today it must be considered in crisis. The reason for the crisis is simply that writing is being supplanted by images—a new medium is being added to the old and taking priority over it in the culture. Flusser understands this change in media in several ways. From a historical point of view (and there is some degree of irony in Flusser's reliance on history for periodizing media changes), image culture begins with the photograph.[14] As technically produced images, photographs encourage a nonlinear form of composition and reading. They "are dams placed in the way of the stream of history, jamming historical happenings."[15] The temporality of reading photographs is an all-at-onceness, not a linear progression. Written texts are decoded in a linear fashion, in a sequence of steps that are narrative in nature, moving from start to finish. According to Flusser, the process of interpreting images is different: "In pictures we may get the message first, and then try to decompose it. . . . This difference is one of temporality, and involved the present, the past and the future."[16] The "historical time" of the written text induces a directional sense in the reader, a feeling of going somewhere, whereas images are read with no sense of movement, with a feeling of going nowhere.

In their composition, as well, Flusser regards photographs as different from writing because they rely on a "calculating, formal" type of thinking.[17] Yet for him, photographs are not a throwback to prehistoric times. There is no identity between photographs and cave paintings, for instance. The latter are mimetic, whereas photographs "are computed possibilities (models, projections onto the environment)."[18]

Flusser is perhaps least convincing in his insistence on the difference between prehistoric images and photographs. Even if photographs have the formal property of "models," one might say the same about cave paintings. And even if cave paintings are in the first instance mimetic, one might easily argue that photographs, at least until the advent of digital technology, have had a mimetic quality as well. Certainly in the culture at large of the nineteenth century, photographs were in good part regarded as indexical. To make Flusser's argument more convincing, one might analyze the difference between the technology of prehistoric images and photography. The difference in the composition process between the two forms of image production is certainly stark. A close reading of *Into the Universe of Technical Images* might help to clarify the distinction for the reader.

In his analysis of the different temporalities of writing and images, Flusser develops a theory of the visual. Writing and images are as different as lines and surfaces. The former, as we have seen, produces historical society, the latter "telematic society." Flusser describes this new world as follows: "The telematic society would be the first to recognize the production of information as society's actual function, and so to systematically foster this production: the first self-conscious and therefore free society."[19] In a somewhat utopian vein, Flusser foresees revolutionary changes when digital images replace first text and then analog images (television, photography, cinema). He imagines, as well, the end of the reign of the author, very much like Foucault and Barthes. He writes, "For genuinely disciplined, theorized creativity will only be possible after the myth of the author of information is abandoned."[20] For Flusser, computer-generated images require a level of creativity unknown in the past, when copying nature was the goal of image production.

The cultural study of media is hampered by a philosophical tradition based on the *episteme* of the transcendental, unconditional, and contextless "I think." From Kant (time as a synthetic a priori of reason) to Husserl (time as a feature of consciousness as it appears to thought) and even to Bergson (time as duration), the nature of time is deduced from logic. A change comes with Derrida and the association of time with the technology of writing, but here again, writing becomes a form (*différance*) inherent to all media and thereby divorced from technological specificity and social practice. Stiegler, in his three-volume work *Technics and Time,* attempts to break from this tradition by inserting technology more firmly within the conceptual formation of time. In his essay "Derrida and Technology" as well as in his televised debate with Derrida, published as a transcripted book titled *Echographies,* Stiegler complains that when Derrida theorizes writing as "archewriting," he places technology in a register of temporality that loses the specificity of different media: "All [media for Derrida]," he writes, "are figures . . . of origin that arche-writing constitutes."[21] Time is thus possible for Stiegler (as for Flusser) through the technical inscription of cultural objects. Wrestling with the question of the transcendental nature of media temporality, Stiegler concludes on a middle ground of what he calls "a-transcendentality."[22]

In Mark Hansen's review of volume 1 of *Technics and Time,* he points out that Stiegler's discovery of the discreteness of the digital image leads him to posit media as constituting subjects in different forms of the awareness of time.[23] Photography, film, and networked computing thus construct distinctly different forms of temporality in the subject. Yet Stiegler, rigorous and systematic in his thinking, still maintains a kind of original disposition of media as material forms of memory, as prostheses. The question that remains open in his work, and that provides a fruitful intersection with Flusser's media theory, is the degree of determination one would give to this primary or initial prosthetic figure. I argue that one must theorize time and media in such a way that the relation is not entirely dependent on the human as ground but instead opens a more complex possibility for multiple assemblages of the human and the machine, not as prostheses *for* the human but as mixtures of human–machine in which the outcome or specific forms of the relation are not prefigured in the initial conceptualization of the relation. Contingency of the relation must be kept open. In that way, the different cultural forms of media and time would each have their own validity, and the critical question of how to institute the newer relation in networked computing would remain an open political question.

Given the importance of the question of media, and of Flusser's work in this area, it is disappointing that the major cultural theorists of the 1970s and 1980s tend to overlook media theory and almost completely ignore the thought of Flusser. Let us take a brief glance at some examples of this lack and this problem.

Michel Foucault provides an interesting example of the problem that also persists in Derrida's work, as we have seen. Foucault's work of the 1970s is densely sprinkled with metaphors of media. *Discipline and Punish* and *The History of Sexuality, Volume 1,* centrally rely on such figures as "technology of power" and "networks," in which individuals are understood as "nodes." His understanding of the individual or subject as constituted by and living within networks in everyday life is highly suggestive for an understanding of the role of media. Similarly, his depiction of the confessional as a peculiar space of speech in early modern France moves very close to an analysis of one form of language in relation to subject positions. Even more, his enigmatic depiction of a world beyond the author function suggests the types of exchanges that prevailed on the Internet before the phenomenon of global communication actually existed:

> All discourses . . . would then develop in the anonymity of a murmur. We would no longer hear the questions that have been rehashed for so long: Who really spoke? Is it really he and not someone else? With what authenticity or original-ity? And what part of his deepest self did he express in his discourse? Instead there would be other questions, like these:

> What are the modes of existence of this discourse? Where has
> it been used, how can it circulate, and who can appropriate
> it for himself? What are the places in it where there is room
> for possible subjects? Who can assume these various subject
> functions? And behind all these questions, we would hear
> hardly anything but the stirring of an indifference: What
> difference does it make who is speaking?[24]

Here Foucault seems to anticipate the world of chat rooms, e-
mail, blogs, and Web pages, where authorship is always in question.
He seems to depict, and even desire, a space of communication
where identity may be in doubt and subordinated to the flow of
text, to the impulses of creativity. And yet the word *media* is absent
from the vocabulary of the critic of authorship. In the end, however,
aside from passing comments on the importance of writing in
the care of self, Foucault does not theorize media as a significant
domain of what he calls "subjectivation."

Then there is Jacques Lacan, whose work has stimulated the
important writings of Slavoj Žižek but whose own work on media
provides perhaps the most egregious examples of the problem I am
addressing. In his widely read (and viewed) television interview
purportedly about television and published in transcript form as
Television, Lacan demonstrates quite clearly that he has, I am sorry
to report, not a whiff of understanding about media. Complain-
ing that the rebellious Parisian students of May 1968 were acting
without a shred of guilt or shame, Lacan argues in *Seminar XVII*
that the young people have symbolically slain their parents because
they have failed to recognize the authority of the gaze of the Other.
Thus they cannot come under the Law, or become subjects of desire
through the good graces of the master signifier, and so on. The
important point in this stunning application of psychoanalysis to
media is that Lacan attributes this moral transgression to television.
Why? Because with television, there is a voice but no individual.[25]
The obvious question is, how is television different from radio,

film, or the Internet, which also emit voices without the speaker's presence? Indeed, books, newspapers—all forms of print—might be included in the list, although in these cases, "voice" is not accompanied by sound. Why, then, limit the complaint to television? Clearly media studies will not be well informed by psychoanalysis if Lacan is any guide.[26]

Gilles Deleuze provides another variation of the absence of media in twentieth-century theory. The seminal, even magisterial works he composed with Félix Guattari, *Anti-Oedipus* and *A Thousand Plateaus,* explore critically the social and cultural space of modernity without mention of media. Their absence threatens to undermine what is otherwise a compelling rethinking of Western reality. The same may be said of Deleuze's two volumes on film.[27] The one exception within Deleuze's considerable and weighty corpus is the short essay "Postscript on Control Societies" (1990),[28] whose title suggests its marginal position in his thought. In the English-speaking discursive community, thinkers have so yearned for a discussion of media that this slight piece has gained attention and praise far exceeding its modest standing. Because of its celebrity, if for no other reason, it is worthy of attention.

In this brief piece, Deleuze emphasizes the absence of confining spatial arrangements in the exercise of domination afforded by the use of computer technology. "What has changed," in the formulation of Deleuze's argument by Hardt and Negri, "is that, along with the collapse of the institutions, the disciplinary *dispositifs* have become less limited and bounded spatially in the social field. Carceral discipline, school discipline, factory discipline, and so forth interweave in a hybrid production of subjectivity."[29] Beyond the negative trait of the absence of "major organizing sites of confinement,"[30] control societies are, in this text, maddeningly undefined. Deleuze discusses the control society again in "Having an Idea in Cinema"[31] but is again both brief and vague, only adding to his previous discussion that because "information is precisely the system of control,"[32] "counterinformation" becomes a form of resistance,[33] all of which suggests to me that Deleuze's understanding of networked digital information machines remains rudimentary. It is hard to imagine what counterinformation might be, for example. Does he mean that critical content is resistance? Or does the form of the critical content constitute resistance?

It might seem logical to conclude from the opposition between societies of discipline and societies of control that Deleuze places himself against Foucault, or at least that he is going beyond Foucault by discerning forms of domination unthought by the historian of the Panopticon. Yet such is not at all the case. Instead, Deleuze proclaims his agreement with Foucault, citing William Burroughs again as the fulcrum of the matter. Deleuze writes, "Foucault agrees with Burroughs who claims that our future will be controlled rather than disciplined."[34] But Deleuze gives no evidence that Foucault anticipated a transformation to societies of control, relegating discipline to the garbage can of history. It would appear that Deleuze was unwilling to position himself as the thinker who went beyond Foucault even as, in the same paragraph, Deleuze compellingly characterizes the break between the two orders of domination. In the following passage, Deleuze insists that Foucault adopts the notion of societies of control: "The disciplines which Foucault describes are the history of what we gradually cease to be, and our present-day reality takes on the form of dispositions of overt and continuous *control* in a way which is very different from recent closed disciplines."[35]

Deleuze's stadial theory, moving from discipline to control, is also far too linear in character. Elements of control existed in Europe in the early modern period as the state hired spies to keep track of suspected miscreants. Equally, forms of discipline proliferate in the twenty-first century as the United States, for example, erects more and more prisons under the so-called get tough policies of recent and current administrations. The shift from discipline to control is also Eurocentric, overlooking the very different disposition of these state strategies in the southern hemisphere. François

Vergès points out, for example, that "in postcolonial Reunion, these two strategies have concurrently occurred. New types of sanction, education, and care have constructed a web of control around the Creoles, and along with the creation of a vast social network of control, there has been a multiplication of prisons, a criminalization and psychologization of politics."[36] Deleuze's model of control as the next stage after discipline thus contains problems at numerous levels.

In an essay from 1998, Michael Hardt attempts to explicate the concept of societies of control beyond what Deleuze has given us. He asserts that as the chief new form of power, "the metaphorical space of the societies of control is perhaps best characterized by the shifting desert sands, where positions are continually swept away; or better, the smooth surfaces of cyberspace, with its infinitely programmable flows of codes and information."[37] Smooth surfaces are opposed to striated planes, categories one recalls from *A Thousand Plateaus*[38] that designate homogeneous and heterogeneous spaces, respectively.[39] But Hardt overlooks the side of cyberspace that resists the power formation of the control society, all kinds of spaces in which copyright law, fixed identities, censorship, and so forth, are continuously evaded and challenged. Cyberspace is hardly Hardt's smooth surface of transparency and control but is rather a highly differentiated field of resistance, conflict, and uncertainty.

For Hardt, control societies are "smooth" because civil society has collapsed, rendering the social lacking in mediations.[40] Hardt analyzes the dialectic of civil society from Hegel to Foucault, concluding that "what has come to an end, or more accurately declined in importance in post–civil society, then, are precisely these functions of mediation or education and the institutions that gave them form."[41] Foucault's disciplinary institutions have lost their ability to position and give identity to individuals. Replacing the spaces of confinement, according to Hardt, are the media. But again, one must object: the media are also mediating, albeit in a different form from older establishments like education and the family. What is lacking in Hardt's understanding of the move from discipline to control is precisely an analysis of media as technologies of power. Surely media are different from prisons, education, and so forth, but one must understand the specificity of media as structuring systems as well as pay attention to the differences of one medium from another. Television, print, and the Internet are each a disciplinary institution—in this sense, they are different from each other but also similar to prisons in that they construct subjects, define identities, position individuals, and configure cultural objects. True enough, media do not require spatial arrangements in the manner of workshops and prisons, but humans remain fixed in space and time: at the computer, in front of the television set, walking or bicycling through city streets, or riding on a subway with headphones and an MP3 player or cell phone. I refer to this configuration of the construction of the subject as a *superpanopticon* to indicate its difference from modern institutions.[42] The term *control society* bears the disadvantage of losing an ability to capture the new technologies of power: the media.

At a more general level, what stands in the way of an approach to media theory for Deleuze is his understanding of film as art. From *Difference and Repetition* to the cinema books of the 1980s, Deleuze frames cinema only as art. When he recognizes the altered sphere of everyday life as steeped in audio and visual technologies, he finds in art a liberatory escape from the quotidian: "The more our daily life appears standardized, stereotyped and subject to an accelerated reproduction of objects of consumption, the art must be injected into it."[43] One cannot come near the problem of media with a view of the everyday as degraded, debased, and baleful.

Perhaps a turn to Flusser will change the disregard for media that has so characterized cultural theory of the 1970s, 1980s, and 1990s. Flusser, however flamboyant and polemical his writing can be, thought deeply about the emergence of electronic media and their implications not only for Western culture but also truly for global culture.

Notes

1   Matthew Fuller, *Media Ecologies: Materialist Energies in Art and Technoculture* (Cambridge, Mass.: MIT Press, 2005).

2   Francis Bacon, *The Advancement of Learning* (London: Cassell, 1893), book 1, chap. 5, para. 11.

3   Vilém Flusser, *Writings* (Minneapolis: University of Minnesota Press, 2002), 1.

4   Friedrick Kittler, "Perspective and the Book," *Grey Room* 5 (2001): 39.

5   Friedrick Kittler, *Discourse Networks: 1800/1900* (Palo Alto, Calif.: Stanford University Press, 1990).

6   Giambattista Vico, *The New Science* (Ithaca, N.Y.: Cornell University Press, 1984).

7   Flusser, *Writings*, 39.

8   Ibid.

9   Katherine Hayles, *Writing Machines* (Cambridge, Mass.: MIT Press, 2002).

10 Ibid., 39.

11 Flusser, *Writings*, 63.

12 Dominick LaCapra, *History and Memory after Auschwitz* (Ithaca, N.Y.: Cornell University Press, 1988).

13 Jacques Derrida and Bernhard Stiegler, *Echographies de la télévision: entretiens filmés* (Paris: Institut national de l'autovisuel, 1996).

14 Vilém Flusser, *Towards a Philosophy of Photography* (Gottingen, Germany: European Photography, 1984).

15 Flusser, *Writings*, 127.

16 Ibid., 23.

17 Ibid., 128.

18 Ibid., 129.

19 Vilém Flusser, *Into the Universe of Technical Images* (Minneapolis: University of Minnesota Press, 2011), 92.

20 Ibid., 101.

21 Jacques Derrida and Bernhard Stiegler, *Echographies of Television* (London: Polity, 2002), 239.

22 B. Stiegler, "Our Ailing Institutions," *Culture Machine* XX (1993).

23 Mark Hansen, "'Realtime Synthesis' and the Différance of the Body: Technocultural Studies in the Wake of Deconstruction," *Culture Machine* XX (2004).

24 Michel Foucault, "What Is an Author?" in *The Foucault Reader,* ed. P. Rabinow (New York: Pantheon, 1984), 119–20.

25 Jacques Lacan, *Television* (New York: W. W. Norton, 1990), 27.

26 Sigmund Freud, *Civilization and Its Discontents* (New York: W. W. Norton, 1961), 39, also manifests a deep unconcern for media. In his famous example of the telephone, he quips that it provides no more satisfaction than sticking one's leg out from under the covers on a cold winter night just to be able to return it to comfort and warmth afterward. For a very different view of the value of Lacan's insights on television, see Rosalind Morris, "The War Drive: Image Files Corrupted," *Social Text* 25, no. 2 (2007): 103–42.

27 Gilles Deleuze, *Cinema 1: The Movement-Image* (Minneapolis: University of Minnesota Press, 1986).

28 Gilles Deleuze, "Postscript on Control Societies," in *Negotiations: 1972–1980* (New York: Columbia University Press, 1990), 177–82.

29 Michael Hardt and Antonio Negri, *Empire* (Cambridge, Mass.: Harvard University Press, 2000), 330.

30 Gilles Deleuze, *Negotiations: 1972–1990* (New York: Columbia University Press, 1995), 177.

31 Gilles Deleuze, "Having an Idea in Cinema," in *Deleuze and Guattari: New Mappings in Politics, Philosophy, and Culture*, ed. Eleanor Kaufman and Kevin Heller (Minneapolis: University of Minnesota Press, 1998), 14–19.

32 Ibid., 17.

33 Ibid., 18.

34 Gilles Deleuze, "What Is a *Dispositif?*" in *Michel Foucault Philosopher,* ed. François Ewald (New York: Routledge, 1992), 164.

35 Ibid.

36 François Vergès, *Monsters and Revolutionaries: Colonial Family Romance and Métissage* (Durham, N.C.: Duke University Press, 1999), 219.

37 Michael Hardt, "Withering of Civil Society," *Social Text* 45 (Winter 1995): 32.

38 Gilles Deleuze and Félix Guattari, *A Thousand Plateaus: Capitalism and Schizophrenia* (Minneapolis: University of Minnesota Press, 1987).

39 Ibid.

40 Hardt, "Withering of Civil Society."

41 Ibid., 36.

42 Mark Poster, *The Mode of Information: Poststructuralism and Social Context* (Chicago: University of Chicago Press, 1990).

43 Gilles Deleuze, *Difference and Repetition,* trans. Paul Patton (New York: Columbia University Press, 1994), 293.

Into the Universe of Technical Images

Warning

With the ideas presented here, I am attempting to follow up a bit more closely on trends noticeable in contemporary technical images such as photographs or television images. In the process, I raise the prospect of a future society that synthesizes electronic images. Seen from here and now, it will be a fabulous society, where life is radically different from our own. Current scientific, political, and artistic categories will hardly be recognizable there, and even our state of mind, our existential mood, will take on a new and strange coloration. This is not about a future floating in the far distance. We are already on its cusp. Many aspects of this fabulous new social and life structure are already visible in our environment and in us. We live in a utopia that is appearing, pushing its way up into our surroundings and into our pores. What is happening around us and in us is fantastic, and all previous utopias, whether they were positive or negative, pale in comparison to it. That is what the following essay is about.

Utopia means groundlessness, the absence of a point of reference. We face the immediate future directly, unequivocally, except inasmuch as we cling to those structures generated by utopia itself. That is what has happened in this essay: it clings to contemporary technical images, it criticizes them. In this sense, it represents a continuation and amendment of those arguments articulated in an earlier essay, *Towards a Philosophy of Photography.*[1] Therefore this essay is to be read not, or not primarily, as the projection of a fantasy into the future but rather as a critique of the present—even though the critique will be caught up in a sense of the inevitability and superior force of the new.

Taking contemporary technical images as a starting point, we find two divergent trends. One moves toward a centrally programmed, totalitarian society of image receivers and image administrators, the other toward a dialogic, telematic society of image producers and image collectors. From our standpoint, both these social structures are fantastic, even though the first presents a somewhat negative, the second a positive, utopia. In any case, we are still free at this point to challenge these values. What we can no longer challenge is the dominance of technical images in this future society. Assuming that no catastrophe occurs (and this is by definition impossible to predict), it is likely—bordering on certain—that the existential interests of future men and women will focus on technical images.

This gives us the right and the duty to call this emerging society a utopia. It will no longer be found in any place or time but in imagined surfaces, in surfaces that absorb geography and history. The following essay seeks to grasp this dreaming state of mind as it has begun to crystallize around technical images: the consciousness of a pure information society.

This cautionary preface was written after the work was completed, as it is in most cases. It comes to some extent in the wake of the experiences and dangers of the journey just completed into the land of our children and grandchildren. That's why it's a warning: one should expect questions rather than answers from the following essay, even when these questions occasionally dress themselves up as answers. To put it another way, this essay does not attempt to suggest some sort of solution to the problems that confront us but rather to critically challenge the fundamental tendencies on which these problems rest.

To Abstract

This essay is about the universe of technical images, the universe that for the past few decades has been making use of photographs, films, videos, television screens, and computer terminals to take over the task formerly served by linear texts, that is, the task of transmitting information crucial to society and to individuals. It is concerned with a cultural revolution whose scope and implications we are just beginning to suspect. Since human beings depend for their lives more on learned and less on genetic information than do other living things, the structure through which information is carried exerts a decisive influence on our lives. When images supplant texts, we experience, perceive, and value the world and ourselves differently, no longer in a one-dimensional, linear, process-oriented, historical way but rather in a two-dimensional way, as surface, context, scene. And our behavior changes: it is no longer dramatic but embedded in fields of relationships. What is currently happening is a mutation of our experiences, perceptions, values, and modes of behavior, a mutation of our being-in-the-world.

Linear texts have only occupied their dominant position as bearers of critically important information for about four thousand years. Only that time, then, can be called "history" in the exact sense of the word. Before that, during the forty-thousand-year period of so-called prehistory, other media—especially pictures—carried this information. And even during the relatively brief period when texts were dominant, images continued to be effective, dialectically challenging the dominance of texts. And so one is tempted to say that linear texts have played only an ephemeral role in the life of

5

human beings, that "history" was only a diversion, and that we are now in the process of turning back to two-dimensionality, into the imaginary, magical, and mythical. Many aspects of emerging life structures, for example, the magic that flows from technical images or the magic-ritual behavior of those knowledgeable about technical images, appear to confirm this view.

The present essay intends to show that this view is incorrect. It maintains that technical images are inherently different from early pictures, which will be referred to here as "traditional." More specifically, technical images rely on texts from which they have come and, in fact, are not surfaces but mosaics assembled from particles. They are therefore not prehistoric, two-dimensional structures but rather posthistorical, without dimension. We are not turning back to a two-dimensional prehistory but rather emerging into a posthistorical, dimensionless state. To support this contention, this chapter proposes a model to be used to clarify the difference in ontological position between traditional and technical images.

The model is a ladder with five rungs. Humanity has climbed this ladder step by step from the concrete toward higher and higher levels of abstraction: a model of cultural history and the alienation of human beings from the concrete.

- *First rung:* Animals and "primitive" people are immersed in an animate world, a four-dimensional space-time continuum of animals and primitive peoples. It is the level of concrete experience.
- *Second rung:* The kinds of human beings that preceded us (approximately two million to forty thousand years ago) stood as subjects facing an objective situation, a three-dimensional situation comprising graspable objects. This is the level of grasping and shaping, characterized by objects such as stone blades and carved figures.
- *Third rung: Homo sapiens sapiens* slipped into an imaginary, two-dimensional mediation zone between itself and its environ-

ment. This is the level of observation and imagining characterized by traditional pictures such as cave paintings.

- *Fourth rung*: About four thousand years ago, another mediation zone, that of linear texts, was introduced between human beings and their images, a zone to which human beings henceforth owe most of their insights. This is the level of understanding and explanation, the historical level. Linear texts, such as Homer and the Bible, are at this level.

- *Fifth rung*: Texts have recently shown themselves to be inaccessible. They don't permit any further pictorial mediation. They have become unclear. They collapse into particles that must be gathered up. This is the level of calculation and computation, the level of technical images.

The intention of the model suggested here is obviously not to diagram cultural history. That would be an absurdly naive undertaking. Rather the model is intended to focus attention on the steps that lead from one level to another. It is meant to show that technical images and traditional images arise from completely different kinds of distancing from concrete experience. It is meant to show that technical images are completely new media, even if they are in many respects reminiscent of traditional images. They "mean" in a completely different way from traditional images. In short, they actually constitute a cultural revolution.

One might object to this model on the grounds that simply to distinguish traditional from technical images, it is not necessary to set up such a broad hypothesis, spanning two million years. It should really be enough to define technical images as those that owe their existence to technical apparatuses. But exactly this definition, obvious as it seems, turns out to be inadequate for the thesis presented here. For I am contending that we can only do justice to the fabulous new way of life that is now emerging around technical images if we delve into the very roots of our being-in-the-world. To be this radical, the proposed model must be this broad.

The five rungs on the ladder that lead from a concrete experience of the environment into the universe of technical images are separated by spaces that must be crossed, crossed in both of the ladder's directions. For each of these crossings, we must exchange one universe for another, and each of them needs now to be considered independently, step by step.

- *First step:* Unlike animals, even primates, human beings have hands that can hold the immediate world at bay, bring it to a stop (so that the environment is no longer relevant). This extension of the hand against the world can be called an "action." With this designation, the lifeworld falls into two areas: the area of the fixed, understood object and the area of the "one who understands," the human subject standing apart from objects, the area of objective conditions and that of the ex-istence of human beings. Action abstracts the subject from the lifeworld, brackets the subject out, and what remains is the three-dimensional universe of graspable objects, the problem to be solved. This universe of objects can now be transformed, informed by the subject. The result is culture.

- *Second step:* Hands do not handle things blindly but are monitored by eyes. The coordination of hand and eye, doing and seeing, practice and theory is a fundamental principle of existence. Circumstances can be observed before they are dealt with. Eyes can see only the surfaces of objects to be grasped, yet eyes command a field that is more comprehensive than that which hands can grasp. And they see the relationships. They can construct models for subsequent actions. The overview that precedes circumstances can be called "worldview." It is about taking a deep measure of circumstances and producing from it a two-dimensional realm of images between the situation and the subject: the universe of traditional images.

- *Third step:* Images stand before things. Man must therefore reach through images to change things. Grasping and acting follow from representational images, and since images are two-dimensional, the representations in them form a circle, that is, one draws its meaning from the other, which in turn lends its meaning to the next. Such a relationship of exchangeable meanings is magical. Grasping and changing the environment through images is magical action. To return to things without mediating through images, to take the magic away from the action, representations must be torn out of the magical context of the pictorial surface and set into another order. The difficulty here is that images aren't graspable. They have no depth; they are only visible. But their surfaces can be grasped with fingers, and fingers that lift representations out of the surface to grasp them can count them and account for them. Linear texts come into being as a result of this gesture called "grasping." Grasping involves a translation from representations into concepts, an explanation of images, an unraveling of pictorial surfaces into lines. This gesture abstracts one dimension from pictorial surfaces, reducing the image to a linear one-dimensionality. The result is a conceptual universe of texts, calculations, narratives, and explanations, projections of an activity that is not magical.

while translation?

- *Fourth step:* Texts are concepts strung together like beads on an abacus, and the threads that order these concepts are rules, orthographic rules. The circumstances described in a text appear by way of these rules and are grasped and manipulated according to them, that is, the structure of the text impresses itself on the circumstances, just as the structure of the image did. Both text and image are "mediations." For a long time, this was not easy to see because the orthographic rules (above all logic and mathematics) produce far more effective actions than the magic that had come before. And we have only recently begun to realize that we don't discover these rules in the environment (e.g., in the form of natural laws); rather they come from our own scientific texts. In this way, we lose faith in the laws of syntax. We recognize in them rules of play that could also be other than they are, and with this recognition, the orderly threads finally fall apart and the concepts lose coherence. In fact, the situation disintegrates into a swarm of particles and quanta, and the writing subject into a swarm of bits and bytes, moments of decision, and molecules of action. What remains are particles without dimension that can be neither grasped nor represented nor understood. They are inaccessible to hands, eyes, or fingers. But they can be calculated (*calculus,* "pebbles") and can, by means of special apparatuses equipped with keys, be computed. The gesture of tapping with the fingertips on the keys of an apparatus can be called "calculate and compute." It makes mosaic-like combinations of particles possible, technical images, a computed universe in which particles are assembled into visible images. This emerging universe, this dimensionless, imagined universe of technical images, is meant to render our circumstances conceivable, representable, and comprehensible. That is the topic to be addressed here.

The difference between traditional and technical images, then, would be this: the first are observations of objects, the second computations of concepts. The first arise through depiction, the second through a peculiar hallucinatory power that has lost its faith in rules. This essay will discuss that hallucinatory power. First, however, imagination must be excluded from the discussion to avoid any confusion between traditional and technical images.

To Imagine

The split in the life world between object and subject happened some two million years ago somewhere in East Africa. About forty thousand years ago, no doubt in a cave in southwestern Europe, the subject withdrew further into its subjectivity to get an overview of the objective circumstances in which it found itself. But at such a remove, things were no longer tangible, manifest, for no hand could reach them anymore. They could only be seen. They were merely appearances—objective circumstances turned into apparent, "phenomenal," and therefore deceptive circumstances: in pursuit of an apparition, hands can miss the object. The subject is once again in doubt about the objectivity of its circumstances, and out of this doubt come observations and images.

Images are intended to serve as models for actions. For although they show only the surfaces of things, they still show relationships among things that no one would otherwise suspect. Images don't show matter; they show what matters. And that allowed the hand to probe further into the circumstances than before. Image makers faced two obstacles, however. First, every observation is subjective, showing one instant from one standpoint, and second, every observation is ephemeral, for the standpoint is in constant motion. If images were to become models for actions, they had to be made accessible, intersubjective, and they had to be stabilized, stored. They had to be "published."

The earliest image makers known to us (e.g., at Lascaux) fixed their observations on the walls of caves to make them accessible to others (to us as well); that is, they acted (for hands are required for this fixing), and did so in a new way, inasmuch as they used their hands not to grasp objects (e.g., bulls) but to manipulate surfaces to represent objects (e.g., bulls). They sought symbols, and the activity was about symbols, about a gesture in which the hands moved back from the object to address the depths of the subject in whom, so stimulated, a new level of consciousness was emerging: the "imaginative." And from this imaginative consciousness came the universe of traditional images, of symbolic content, the universe that would henceforth serve as a model for manipulating the environment (e.g., hunting bulls).

Symbols that are linked to content in this way are called codes and can be deciphered by initiates. To be intersubjective (to be decoded by others), each image must rest on a code known to a community (initiates), which is the reason images are called "traditional" in this essay. Each image must be part of a chain of images, for if it were not in a tradition, it would not be decipherable. Of course, this doesn't necessarily always work. That is what it means to "publish": to put a subjective observation into the symbols of a social code. Of course, it doesn't necessarily work. Because every observation is subjective, each new image brings some sort of new symbol into the code. Each new image will therefore distinguish itself to some small degree from the previous one and so be an original. It will change the social code and inform society. That is just what the power of imagination is: it enables a society informed by images to generate continually new knowledge and experience and to keep reevaluating and responding to it.

Yet it is a dangerous anachronism to regard these constant changes in the image code as a developmental process and to speak of a "history of images" (e.g., from the bull paintings at Lascaux to those of Mesopotamia and Egypt) or to suppose that such a history unfolds slowly in comparison to our own. For what makers of images set out to do was exactly not to be original and to inform society but rather to be as true as possible to previous images and to carry their tradition forward with as little noise as possible.

These makers tried to reduce their subjectivity to a minimum, an attitude that can be observed in so-called prehistoric cultures in the present. The African mask and the Indian textile are concerned with an unchanging, eternal code, a myth. To the extent the mask or the textile is original, it has failed.

The universe of traditional images is a magical and mythical universe, and if it nevertheless changed constantly, this was through unintentional coincidence, by accident. This is a prehistoric universe. Only since linear texts appeared, and with them conceptual, historical consciousness—some four thousand years ago—can one rightly speak of a history of images. For only then did imagination begin to serve (and oppose) conceptual thinking, and only then did image makers concern themselves with being original, with deliberately introducing new symbols, with generating information. Only then was an accident no longer an oversight but rather an insight. Images of our time are infected with texts; they visualize texts. Our image makers' imaginations are infected with conceptual thinking, with trying to hold processes still.

The universe of traditional images, not yet sullied with texts, is a world of magical content. It is a world of the eternal return of the same, in which everything lends meaning to everything else and anything can be meant by anything else. It is a world full of meanings, full of "gods." And human beings experienced this world as one permeated by trouble. That is the imaginative state of mind: everything carries meaning, everything must be appeased. It is a state of guilt and sin.

At first glance, technical images seem similar to the prehistoric images just discussed. But they are on an entirely different level of consciousness, and among them life proceeds in an entirely different atmosphere. Visualization is something completely different from depiction, something radically new, and will now be taken under consideration.

To Make Concrete

According to the suggested model of cultural history, we are about to leave the one-dimensionality of history for a new, dimensionless level, one to be called, for lack of a more positive designation, "posthistory." The rules that once sorted the universe into processes, concepts into judgments, are dissolving. The universe is disintegrating into quanta, judgments into bits of information. In fact, the rules are dissolving exactly because we followed them into the core of both the universe and our own consciousness. At the core of the universe, particles no longer follow the rules (e.g., chain reactions) and begin to buzz, and at the core of consciousness, we try to sift out the calculable basis of our thinking, feeling, and desire (e.g., proposition theory, decision theory, and the calculation of behavior in actemes); that is, linearity is decaying spontaneously, and not because we decided to throw away the rules. And so we have no choice but to risk a leap into the new.

And it is truly a risk. For as waves dissolve into drops, judgments into bytes, actions into actemes, a void appears, namely, the void of the intervals that hold the elemental points apart and the no-dimensionality and so impossibility of measuring the points themselves. One cannot live in such an empty and abstract universe, with such a dissociated and abstract consciousness. To live, one must try to make the universe and consciousness concrete. One must try to consolidate the particles to make them substantial (graspable, conceivable, tangible). Those who invented calculus in the seventeenth century already solved this problem of filling in the intervals, integrating the infinitesimal, resolving differentials. But at the time, the problem was methodological, and today, it has become existential, a question of life and death. I suggest that we regard technical images as an answer to this problem.

Technical images arise in an attempt to consolidate particles around us and in our consciousness on surfaces to block up the intervals between them in an attempt to make elements such as photons or electrons, on one hand, and bits of information, on the other hand, into images. This can be achieved neither with hands nor with eyes nor with fingers, for these elements are neither graspable, nor are they visible. For this reason, apparatuses must be developed that grasp the ungraspable, visualize the invisible, and conceptualize the inconceivable. And these apparatuses must be fitted with keys so that we may manipulate them. These apparatuses are essential for the production of technical images. All the rest comes later.

Apparatuses are intractable; they should not be anthropomorphized, however convincingly they may simulate human thought functions. They have no trouble with particles. They want neither to grasp nor to represent nor to understand them. To an apparatus, particles are no more than a field of possible ways in which to function. What we find difficult to see (e.g., a magnetic field, unless we use iron filings) is, from its standpoint, just another possible function. It transforms the effects of photons on molecules of silver nitrate into photographs in just the same way: blindly. And that is what a technical image is: a blindly realized possibility, something invisible that has blindly become visible.

The production of technical images occurs in a field of possibilities: in and of themselves, the particles are nothing but possibilities from which something accidentally emerges. "Possibility" is, in other words, the stuff of the universe and the consciousness that is emerging. "We are such stuff as dreams are made on."[1] The two horizons of the possible are "inevitable" and "impossible"; in the direction of the inevitable, the possible becomes probable; in the impossible direction, it becomes improbable. So the basis for the emerging universe and emerging consciousness is the calculation of probability. From now on, concepts such as "true" and "false" refer only to unattainable horizons, bringing a revolution not only in the field of epistemology but also in those of ontology, ethics, and aesthetics.

"Probable" and "improbable" are concepts from informatics, in which information can be defined as an improbable situation: the more improbable, the more informative. The second law of thermodynamics suggests that the emerging particle universe tends toward an increasingly probable situation, toward disinformation, that is, to a steadily more even distribution of particles, until form is finally lost altogether. The last stage, heat death, is a probability bordering on the inevitable, and this stage can be calculated in advance with a probability bordering on certainty.

For the time being, however, we are not at this stage. On the contrary, everywhere in the universe, we can observe that improbable situations have arisen and continue to arise, whether these are galactic spirals, living cells, or human brains. Such informative situations owe their existence to an improbable coincidence, an "erroneous" exception to the general rule of increasing entropy. This permits the following fantastic hypothesis: a sufficiently large computer could, theoretically, futurize (retroactively calculate) all the improbable situations that have already appeared, are about to appear, or are yet to appear, that is, everything between the big bang and heat death, including the text that is taking shape here and including the computer itself. To do this, the computer must have the program of the big bang in its memory. The difficulty for the construction of such a computer is not the literally astronomical quantity of possibilities that surround such situations as spiral nebula, living cells, or human brains; rather the difficulty lies in the necessity for the computer to contain not only the big bang program itself but also all the errors in this program. In other words, it would have to be much larger than the universe itself, an example of the abyss into which the new calculating and computing consciousness is about to fall.

Such dizzying speculations nevertheless permit a closer look at the intentions with which image-making mechanisms were invented, namely, to produce improbable, informative situations to consolidate invisible possibilities into visible improbabilities. As a result, such mechanisms contain programs that contravene the program of the particle universe. For an apparatus is a human product, and a human being is an entity that actively opposes the implacable tendency of the universe toward disinformation. Since a human being stretched out his hand to confront the lifeworld, to make it pause, he has been trying to imprint information on his surroundings. His answer to "heat death" and to death per se is to "inform." And apparatuses, among other things, arose from this, his search for eternal life. They are meant to produce, store, and distribute information. Seen in this way, technical images are reservoirs of information that serve our immortality.

But there is a strange inner dialectic, a contradiction in this undertaking. The apparatus is programmed to generate improbable situations. This means that such improbable situations are in their programs and do not arise as errors, as in the program of the universe, but as situations that are deliberately sought, that become more probable as the program runs. Someone who knows the program of an apparatus can predict these situations and so has no need of a metaphysical computer such as that described in the dizzying speculation introduced earlier. Anyone who watches television can more or less predict the program of the next few weeks. To put this another way: those images produced by an apparatus in keeping with its program are improbable from the standpoint of the universe (it would take billions of years for a photograph to make itself, without an apparatus), but from the receiver's standpoint, they are still probable, which is to say not very informative. For the receiver of technical images, then, that which was programmed into the apparatus as negative entropy is transformed into entropy—just as surreptitiously.

The inherent contradiction in the apparatus arises because it functions just as the universe does, namely, automatically. Its programs are games in which possibilities occur randomly, programmed accidents. The difference between the apparatus and the universe is that the apparatus continues with its programmed tasks (e.g., with a photograph made by a fully automated satellite camera), and the universe runs past the programmed task toward heat death. For this is, in fact, the definition of *automation:* a self-governing computation of accidental events, excluding human intervention and stopping at a situation that human beings have determined to be informative. The difference between the apparatus and the universe is, accordingly, that the apparatus is subject to human control. But it cannot stay this way forever: in the longer term, the autonomy of the apparatus must be liberated from human beings. This is why the negative entropy of the apparatus changes to entropy.

The danger that lurks in automation, namely, that the apparatus will continue, even when the intended result has been achieved, to unintended results (as, say, the apparatus of thermonuclear armaments), is the real challenge to the producer of technical images. Such producers will be called "envisioners" here to distinguish them from those who produce traditional images and to differentiate between visualization and depiction. These are people who press the keys of an apparatus to make it stop at an intentionally informative situation, people determined to control the apparatus in spite of its tendency to become more and more automated and so to preserve human judgment over the machine. Envisioners are people who try to turn an automatic apparatus against its own condition of being automatic. They cannot create illusions without the automatic apparatus, for the stuff to be envisioned, the particles, are neither visible nor graspable nor comprehensible without the apparatus's keys. But they can't turn the envisioning over to the automatic apparatus either, for the technical images produced in such a way would be redundant, that is, predictable, uninformative situations from the standpoint of the apparatus's program.

The task set by the inner contradictions of an automatic apparatus is itself contradictory. For example, if we look at the gesture of a photographer with his camera and compare it with the movements of a fully automatic camera (as in a satellite), we are tempted to underestimate the task. For it looks as though the fully automatic camera is always tripped by chance, whereas the photographer only presses the release when he approaches a situation that corresponds to his intentions. But if we look more closely, we can confirm that the photographic gesture, in fact, does somehow carry out the apparatus's inner instructions. The apparatus does as the photographer desires, but the photographer can only desire what the apparatus can do. Any image produced by a photographer must be within the program of the apparatus and will be, in keeping with the considerations outlined earlier, a predictable, uninformative image. That is to say, then, that not only the gesture but also the intention of the photographer is a function of the apparatus. And yet fully automatic photography can be clearly distinguished from the photography of someone who visualizes an image because in the second case, a human intention works against the autonomy of the apparatus from the inside, from the automatic function itself.

The gesture on which technical images depend is doubly contradictory. First, apparatuses are supposed to generate informative situations automatically. In the face of this contradiction, envisioners try to pit automatic production against the machine's autonomy, an effort that itself occurs within the automatic apparatus. Technical images result from a gesture that is doubly self-involved, from an intricate opposition and collaboration between the inventor and the manipulator of the apparatus and an opposition and collaboration between an apparatus and a human being.

In comparing this gesture with that of traditional images (as described in the previous chapter), it becomes clear that the two occur at two completely different levels. With technical images, it is about first programming the computation of particles, then deprogramming them to convert them into informative situations. It is about a gesture that takes place in a particle universe, with fingertips touching keys, and the structure of this gesture is as particulate as the structure of the universe, that is, it consists of clear and distinct mini-gestures. The intention of this gesture is to make particles into two-dimensional images, to rise from no dimensions to two dimensions, from the abyss of intervals to the surface, from the most abstract into the apparently concrete. "Apparently," for it is, in fact, impossible to gather particles into surfaces. Since every surface is composed of infinitely many particles, an infinity of points would have to be assembled to produce actual surfaces. Therefore the envisioner can produce only a virtual image, that is, a surface full of intervals, like a raster. The envisioner must be content with the appearance of surface, with trompe l'oeil.

The gesture of the envisioner is directed from a particle toward a surface that can never be achieved, whereas that of the traditional image maker is directed from the world of objects toward an actual surface. The first gesture attempts to make concrete (to turn from extreme abstraction back into the imaginable); the second abstracts (retreats from the concrete). The first gesture starts with a calculation; the second starts with a solid object. In short, we are concerned here with two image surfaces that are conceived completely differently, opposed to one another, even though they appear to blend together (something like dermis and epidermis). So when we speak about the meaning of images, about decoding them, we need to be aware that the meaning of technical images is to be sought in a place other than that of traditional images.

The decoding of technical images is a task we have not yet accomplished, for reasons to be discussed further later. But as long as we remain incapable of doing this, we remain at the mercy of a fascination and programmed to engage in magical-ritual behavior. The critical reception of technical images demands a level of consciousness that corresponds to the one in which they are produced. This poses the question whether we as a society are capable of such a change of consciousness. To keep this question in mind, we need to reflect on our contemporary being-in-the-world, our contemporary mode of behavior.

To Touch

Having disintegrated into particles, all recognizable orientation points having become abstract, the world is now to be gathered together so that we may again experience it, recognize it, act in it. This is what envisioners do. Yet the particles that need gathering are neither visible nor graspable nor comprehensible. They can only be grasped with the help of instruments capable of reaching into the mass of particles. These instruments are called "keys." Although we've long been familiar with keys and use them for the most part without thinking, we're still a long way from understanding them. If we want to gain some insight into the world in which we find ourselves when we press keys with our fingertips, we must look more closely at the matter of pushing keys.

Keys are everywhere. Light switches illuminate dark rooms in an instant. The car engine springs to life the instant a key turns, and one press of a shutter release instantly causes an image to be made. What is immediately striking about it all is that the keys operate in a time unrelated to everyday human time, a time that follows another set of standards. For the keys move in the infinitesimal universe of particles, in the realm of the infinitely small, where time ignites like lightning. The second thing about keys is that being infinitely small by human standards, they can also cross over into the gigantic. One flick of the light switch crosses from the universe of electrons into the area in which man is the measure of all things. And one flick of another switch can explode a mountain or finish humanity off. Keys are, accordingly, instruments that bridge the famous sandwich, according to which the world is made up of three layers, one with atomic, one with human, and one with astronomical dimensions.

Often the keys are not isolated buttons but make up keyboards, offering a selection. If I choose a particular button on the control panel of my television, the image I have selected from those available to me appears instantly on the screen. In spite of the inhumanly small dimension with which the keys operate, they still serve human freedom. Even the generation that did not grow up with computer keyboards can still experience what is ghostly and magical about them. As I run my fingertips selectively over the keyboard of my typewriter to write this text, I achieve a miracle. I break my thoughts up into words, words into letters, and then select the keys that correspond to these letters. I calculate my ideas. And the letters then appear on the piece of paper that has been put into the typewriter, each for itself, clear and distinct, and nevertheless forming a linear text. The typewriter computes what I have calculated. It succeeds in packaging the particles into rows. That is a miracle, despite the transparency of the process. For I can watch as each pressed key sets a hammer in motion that strikes the intended letter onto the page and how the carriage moves to make way for the next letter. Despite this transparency, the thing is not right.

Such mechanical typewriters have archaic keyboards. With word processors, writing by pressing keys has long since become an opaque process, an event that occurs in a black box to which the presser has no visual access. An apparatus is not a machine, and its mechanical aspects have disappeared. By observing how images are synthesized on a computer screen by pressing keys, we can, looking back in a sense, recognize the miracle of mechanical button pressing as well: it is the miracle of calculation followed by computation, the miracles to which technical images owe their existence.

The verb *to touch* means first a blind contact, in the hope of finding something by chance: a heuristic method. This is, in fact, the method chimpanzees use to write on the typewriter, the way they will eventually have to produce, by chance, a text identical to this one (in a term projected into the future, potentially encompassing a few million years). I cannot claim, of course, that I experience my own typewriting as blind contact; rather I am persuaded that my text is not the result of an accident that has become unavoidable but that I intentionally select my keys. As I write, I command a "universe of alphanumeric signs" (more than forty-five keys), and for me, each strike is the result of a free decision. One is tempted to claim that I am different from a chimpanzee: that I intentionally reduce the astronomical amount of time that would be required to produce this text by heuristic methods, through chance, to a time on a human scale. I distinguish myself from chimpanzees and other ignorant beings in that I produce the same things they do but in a much shorter time, a sobering account of human freedom and value.

But the matter can be presented differently. Whereas the typing chimpanzee is immersed in a blind play of chance and necessity, I transcend this play. As I type, I see past the game (the typewriter) to the text to be written. I won't yet descend into the problem of freedom, that philosophical quagmire that surrounds this seeing-past-what-is to what-should-be, and will restrict myself to what is. I will therefore ask, is there a possibility that the text written by the chimpanzee could be distinguished from mine, even if they were identical to one another, letter for letter? Is it possible to discover in my text, as opposed to the chimpanzee's, an intention to inform, to establish values? If so, then we could define human freedom and value as the capacity to establish values.

What is at issue here is the difference between human and artificial intelligence, between information that is produced intentionally and automatically. Typewriting chimpanzees are surely extremely primitive artificial intelligences. They are rare, expensive, and slow.

By comparison, word processors are more common, cheaper, and above all much faster. So could we distinguish my text from one produced by a word processor if it matched mine letter for letter? If we ask in this way, it becomes clear that the word processor is not pressing blindly but is programmed. The text is predicted in its program. It doesn't strike purely by chance but casts among the available keys for the rules of a game of chance, not in the sense of a pure but rather of an aleatory chance (*aleae,* "dice"). The word processor's text is a "weighted" game, a predictable accident. Can this controlled result be distinguished from my own text—or is this, too, a weighted game with different programming?

But the chimpanzee, too, plays with dice. It's just that he adheres to very loose rules. He is permitted any combination of keys, and that is exactly why it takes so long for him to arrive at my text. Could one say of the chimpanzee, then, that he is "freer" than the word processor? And the stenographer who copies my text, does he not also throw the dice, only according to far stricter rules, inasmuch as he follows the model before him key for key? So is the chimpanzee engaged in more open and the stenographer in more closed play? Perhaps in this way a hierarchy of programs could be set up, according to the degree to which each is open. As a writer, the chimpanzee is the most free, the stenographer the least free, the word processor somewhere in the middle. But where is my own place in this hierarchy? Am I less free than the chimpanzee but more free than the word processor? And can my position be read from the text? It's an uncomfortable question because it dilutes the specificity of human freedom.

Perhaps the specificity may be rescued from the other direction. For striking a key is, after all, about a pressing on an instrument that has been fabricated by human beings. Wouldn't it be in the making of the keys rather than in the pressing of them, then, that one should seek human freedom? Not in the programmed action, but in the programming? Not in the chimpanzee or the word processor or in the stenographer or in me but rather in the inventor of the typewriter? That would be the one who took Latin letters, Arabic numbers, and a number of logical symbols out of their contexts to turn them into keys, the one who calculated thought processes (took the principles out of them) and then built a machine that could compute these calculations into texts. It doesn't matter very much which type of automaton the inventor of the typewriter built into his machine (whether chimpanzee, word processor, stenographer, or me) or how he programmed this automaton, for in the final analysis, all texts, even mine, must appear on a piece of paper. The specifically human freedom would then be that of programming.

I admit, my typewriter example is mischievous. It is absurd to suggest that the inventor of the typewriter is responsible for the text I am producing. Had I chosen another example—say, television controls—the absurdity would not be so obvious. Most keys are, in fact, like those of the television controls, giving the impression that the programmer is out of sight, pulling the strings of our behavior. To accept that this argument is absurd is to reject a great deal of contemporary cultural criticism.

But the argument that makes programmers responsible for social behavior is completely unacceptable for another reason as well. For backtracking from the key back to the program and from there back to the programmer is a step into the abyss of infinite regress. For example, the chimpanzee and I myself are, just like a typewriter, products of a game of chance, a program. We have both appeared in the course of aleatory play with genetic information. The invention of keys, an event that had necessarily to occur at some point, was in my program but apparently not in the chimpanzee's. Should we look for a programmer behind my program, a superhuman programmer who has to bear responsibility for all the typewriting (mine and the chimpanzee's) and, in fact, for all the world's behavior? For one can't have it both ways—on one hand, the rigid autonomy of keys reaching into the mass of particles, and on the other, a programmed intention—unless one falls head over heels into a belief in the transcendental determinism of chance. In rejecting any such orientalizing faith, one is also forced to reject the argument that social behavior is programmed. Anyone who does not believe in a blindly transcendent programmer is even less likely to believe in a farsighted immanent programmer.

So what is the status of human freedom with respect to writing with a typewriter, with this transparent, mechanical process? Probably as follows: I know, when I strike a key, that I am dealing with a programmed instrument that reaches into the swirl of particles and packages them into texts. I know that a word processor can do this automatically, a chimpanzee can do it accidentally, and a stenographer can do it by copying an existing pattern, and that in all cases, the same text as mine will appear. I know, therefore, that my keys are inviting me into a determined mesh of accident and necessity. And in spite of it all, I experience my writing gesture concretely as a free gesture, in fact, free to such an extent that I would rather give up my life than give up my typewriter. "Writing is necessary, living is not."[1] For my being is concentrated on my fingertips when I am writing: my entire will, thought, and behavior flow into them and through them, past the keys, past the particle universe those keys command, past the typewriter and the paper and into the public sphere. This, my "political freedom," my key-striking, publicizing gesture, is my concrete experience of keys.

An enthusiasm for keys such as the one I have just confessed may be put in the context of the two previous chapters approximately as follows. Action is the first gesture to free human beings from their lifeworld. The second is visual observation. The third is conceptual explanation. And the fourth gesture to free human beings from their lifeworld is the computing touch. The hand makes humankind the subject of the world, the eye makes it the surveyor of the world, fingers make it ruler of the world, and through fingertips, humankind becomes what gives the world meaning. The current cultural revolution can be viewed as a transfer of existence to the fingertips. Work (hand), ideology (eye), and narrative (finger) will be subordinated to programmed computation. In this way, keys will free us from the pressure of changing the world, overseeing it and explaining it, and will free us for the task of giving meaning to the world and life in it.

Of course, this condition, in which keys will free human beings to make meaning, has so far not been reached. Instead we find ourselves being controlled by relatively primitive keys that have not yet been properly understood and therefore not properly installed. For the time being, that is, there are still two types of keys. One type sends messages (call it the "productive" key). The other receives messages (call it the "reproductive" key). The first type is an instrument for making the private public, the other an instrument for making public matters private. For example, the keys of television producers serve to publicize the private views and concepts of the producers, and the keys on the television monitor serve to receive these publicized views and concepts into a private sphere. Both types of keys are, in fact, synchronized with one another, but a double ambience reigns over them: on the sending side is a sense of illusion (that rapture I tried to describe earlier), on the receiving side, a sense of being manipulated (the basis for that kind of cultural criticism I tried previously to discredit).

In considering these two types of keys, one realizes with some surprise that they depend on an obsolete conception and fail to take the actual character of keys into account. They depend, that is, on a conception of "discourse." A message is generated in the private sphere of the sender and is sent through the public sphere and into the private sphere of the receiver. In the example given earlier, the television message is generated in the private space of the producers, sent through public space, and received in the private space of the television audience. But in the universe of keys, there is no longer any private and public. The producer does not generate his message in a private space but rather in a transmitter, a complex of instruments and functionaries. It would be ridiculous to refer to the electromagnetic field through which the message runs as a republic. And the space of the television monitor is open to countless messages and cannot really be called private. Apart from this, the sending and receiving mechanisms are coordinated and function as a unity. In short, keys have burst the boundaries between private and public. They have blended political with private space and made all inherited conceptions of discourse superfluous.

The two types of keys in current use depend therefore on a misunderstanding of what is characteristic of keys. For it is in the character of keys to link up with one another "in dialogue" (e.g., through cables) to form networks, that is, to operate not as discursive but rather as dialogical instruments. The difference between sending and receiving, between productive and reproductive keys, is therefore to be viewed as provisional. The typewriter is only a forerunner of the telewriter, the control panel of the washing machine only a forerunner of a feedback loop linking manufacturers and the users of washing machines. And the current state of keys in general is only a forerunner of a telematic society.

Keys have ruptured our conceptions of political and private space. They force us to think in other categories. In the face of the emerging situation, controlled by dialogically linked keys, we can no longer use concepts like McLuhan's global village. One can no longer speak of a village when there is no public village square and no private houses. The web of keys and dialogic connections between them is more reminiscent of brain structure. One might speak of a global brain rather than a global village. And in such a structure, no distinction can be made between the pressing of a shutter release of the photographic camera and the start button of a washing machine. Both movements receive and send to the same extent.

At the current stage of key development, there will continue to be faulty keys, namely, those that permit me to choose but not to express myself (e.g., the television control panel). For the time being, the freedom to choose therefore contradicts existential freedom. And so for the time being, I cannot become enraptured about the keys on the television or the washing machine (unless I share the rapture of the washing machine user in advertisements for washing machines). But we can expect to be enraptured by all keys at a later stage of automation because they will all be instruments that permit us to join with all others, giving meaning to the whirring chaos of the particulate universe.

Producers of technical images, those who envision (photographers, cameramen, video makers), are literally at the end of history. And in the future, everyone will envision. Everyone will be able to use keys that will permit them, together with everyone else, to synthesize images on the computer screen. They will all be, strictly speaking, at the end of history. The world in which they find themselves can no longer be counted and explained: it has disintegrated into particles—photons, quanta, electromagnetic particles. It has become intangible, inconceivable, incomprehensible, a mass that can be calculated. Even their own consciousness, their thoughts, desires, and values, have disintegrated into particles, into bits of information, a mass that can be calculated. This mass must be computed to make the world tangible, conceivable, comprehensible again, and to make consciousness aware of itself once more. That is to say, the whirring particles around us and in us must be gathered onto surfaces; they must be envisioned.

We already have the visualizing power needed to do this, that is, power over apparatuses we can use to visualize. We know that these apparatuses operate according to principles of chance and necessity (the principles that govern probabilities) and that they operate automatically. And yet at the point of releasing the shutter, we are justifiably convinced that we are giving the whirring and

completely abstract universe around us and in us an intended meaning. That is what is at once ghostly and enticing about envisioning
with keys: technical images are phantoms that can give the world,
and us, meaning.

The following chapter will concern this visualization and the
power to do it, distinguishing it from the imagination of traditional
image making that preceded it. It is about technical images, these
particulate phantoms, these gossamer whims of a cosmic brain in
formation. It proposes to show how surfaces emerge and how a
visionary power is expressed in these surfaces that would never
have been possible before the invention of keys.

To Envision

Technical images are envisioned surfaces. When we look at a photograph with a magnifying glass, we see grains. When we get close to the television screen, we see points. It is true that the photograph is a chemical image and the television an electronic one and that we are dealing with different ways of structuring particles. But the basic construction of particle elements is the same. As long as there are still images that rely on chemistry (presumably not much longer), the way the problem of envisioning presents itself technically (and so also perceptually) in surfaces will be different from the way it presents itself in electronic images. The point is that all technical images have the same basic character: on close inspection, they all prove to be envisioned surfaces computed from particles.

One really does have to observe closely to see this. At first glance, technical images appear to be surfaces. Observing takes more than just looking, which explains why we have insight into hardly any of the many things we see. Technical images seem to be surfaces as a result of our laziness about close observation. This contradiction between looking and observing, between "superficial reading" and "close reading," raises the familiar issue of the distance between the observer and the observed. I will try to show here that technical images are completely different from other objects that make up the objective world around us in terms of the way this issue presents itself.

The wooden table I am using to write this text is, on close observation, a swarm of particles and, for the most part, empty space. Its robust wholeness is an illusion. If my typewriter were to fall through the tabletop, it would be an extremely improbable oc-currence but in no sense a miracle. For this reason, I can bracket all awareness of the granular structure out of my writing and rely on my table's solidity. In the case of the table, the theory follows from practice; that is, the theoretical scientists who have calculated the quantitative structure of my table entered the picture much later and had nothing to do with my table's manufacture.

Yesterday I saw Mozart's opera *Cosi fan tutte* on television. On closer observation, I saw traces of electrons in the cathode ray tube. I cannot bracket out my knowledge of the granular structure of the visible image as I could with the table, however, for I owe this im-age to the theoretical scientists. They alone made yesterday's *Cosi fan tutte* possible. What I actually experienced as beauty yesterday required the calculations and computations of a close reading of the particulate universe. The theory precedes the practice of *Cosi fan tutte,* and without the theory, there can be no practice.

The examples of the table and the video image of *Cosi fan tutte* allow us to formulate what is meant here by the concept of "envision." It is meaningless to claim that the table's solidity is illusory, for it is actually solid, and its particulate composition would only become obvious after this solidity had been subjected to a series of abstrac-tions. On the other hand, one could rightly claim that yesterday, I hallucinated a Mozart opera. For what I saw yesterday followed from a series of concretizations (calculations and computations) of abstract particles, and that is the reason I had a concrete experience yesterday. It was concrete because it had been visualized for me out of abstractions. *Envision,* then, should refer to the capacity to step from the particle universe back into the concrete. I therefore suggest that the power to envision first appeared when technical images were invented. Only since we have had photographs, films, television, videos, and computer screens have we been able to understand what it means to envision.

A closer look at technical images shows that they are not images at all but rather symptoms of chemical or electronic processes. A

photograph shows a chemist how specific molecules of silver com-
pound have reacted to specific photons. A television image shows
a physicist the paths specific electrons have taken in a tube. Read
in this way, technical images are objective depictions of events in
the particle universe. They make these processes visible, just as a
Wilson chamber makes the trace of a particle visible. The objectivity of this visibility does present certain familiar problems for the
theory of perception, however. For since the particle can only be
seen when specific instruments (media) are in use, such as sensi-
tive surfaces, cathode ray tubes, or Wilson chambers, the question
whether these instruments themselves affect the phenomenon they
seek to make visible becomes a problem.

Technical images are only images at all if they are seen superficially. To be images, they require that the viewer keep his distance.
Had a physicist looked closely at yesterday's television image, *Cosi
fan tutte,* he would have seen traces of electrons in the cathode ray
tube. What the physicist's profound insight would have brought to
light is the obdurate banality of the particle universe. I, on the other
hand, having looked only superficially, have actually seen *Cosi van
tutte.* Shall we praise superficiality, praise the power to visualize,
condemn deep insight? "Art is better than truth"?

Incidentally, the theoretical scientists, these people of deep
insight, did not actually produce yesterday's image but only made
it possible. Technicians and envisioners made it, and they are
superficial people. They pressed various buttons and, in so doing,
unleashed processes into which they needed no deep insight, and so
made it possible for me, pressing just as mindlessly on my buttons,
to see *Cosi fan tutte.* What was going on in the various black boxes
that linked me to the envisioners is a question for those with deep
insight. If we are asking about the power to envision, we must let
the black box remain—cybernetically—black.

That is to say, the inquiry into visualization has a strange (and new)
mistrust of deep explanation, resulting in a strange (and new) contempt for depth as such. Scientific explanations and the technologies

that follow from them are essential to the power to visualize, and yet they have become uninteresting. For the explanations arrive at banalities. It is the concrete experience, the adventure, the information that the visualization communicates that is interesting. The explanation is abstract; it is the visualization that is concrete. This is exactly what is new in the emerging power to visualize, what is new about the consciousness that is dawning: scientific discourse and technical progress are seen as essential but no longer interesting in themselves, and we seek adventure elsewhere, in visual constructs.

The inquiry into visualization therefore needs to be transferred from the gesture of the one who presses the buttons to the consciousness of the envisioner, as I tried to do with regard to writing with a typewriter. And there we found that the gesture of pressing buttons is the same in both cases but that envisioning requires a different consciousness. For this is about opaque apparatuses, not transparent machines. Envisioners don't stand over apparatuses the way a writer stands over a typewriter; they stand right in among them, with them, surrounded by them. They are bound much more tightly to the apparatus than a writer to the machine. Envisioning is far more functional than writing texts. It is a programmed procedure. When I write, I write past the machine toward the text. When I envision technical images, I build from the inside of the apparatus.

This condition depends on two factors. First, envisioners press buttons that set events into motion that they cannot grasp, understand, or conceive. Second, the images they visualize are produced not by them but by the apparatus, and, in fact, automatically. In contrast to writers, envisioners have no need for deep insight into what they are doing. By means of the apparatus, they are freed from the pressure for depth and may devote their full attention to constructing images. A writer must concern himself with the structure of a text: for letters; for the rules governing the order in which the letters must appear (orthography, grammar, logic); and for the phonetic, rhythmic, and musical aspects of the text. A large part of his creative, informative achievement consists of his handling of these structures. With the envisioner, it's completely different: he controls an automatic apparatus that brackets all of that out for him so that he is able to concentrate completely on the surface to be envisioned. His criteria as he pushes buttons are therefore superficial in two senses of the word: they have no connection to the more profound craft of constructing an image, and they have no concern with anything beyond the surface to be produced.

The envisioner's superficiality, to which the apparatus has condemned him and for which the apparatus has freed him, unleashes a wholly unanticipated power of invention. Images appear as no one before could ever have dreamed they would. And the photographs, films, and television and video images that surround us at present are only a premonition of what envisioning power will be able to do in the future. Only when we focus on computer-synthesized images, images of the nearly impossible because ungraspable, unimaginable, and incomprehensible, can we start even to suspect what sort of hallucinatory power is at hand.

Envisioners press buttons to inform, in the strictest sense of that word, namely, to make something improbable out of possibilities. They press buttons to seduce the automatic apparatus into making something that is improbable within its program. They press buttons to coax improbable things from the whirring particle universe that the apparatus is calculating. And this improbable world of envisioning power surrounds the whirring particle universe like a skin, giving it a meaning. The power to envision is the power that sets out to make concrete sense of the abstract and absurd universe into which we are falling.

This reflection permits us to define the position of the new consciousness, the power to envision. Envisioners stand at the most extreme edge of abstraction ever reached, in a dimensionless universe, and they offer us the possibility of again experiencing the world and our lives in it as concrete. Only through photographs, films, television, video images, and, in the future, above all, through computer-synthesized images are we able to turn back to concrete experience, recognition, value, and action and away from the world of abstraction from which these things have vanished.

Given what has just been said with respect to envisioning, the current cultural revolution can be summarized roughly as follows. We are the first generation to command the power to envision in the strict sense of the word, and all vision, imagination, and fictions of the past must pale in comparison to our images. We are about to reach a level of consciousness in which the search for deep coherence, explanation, enumeration, narration, and calculation, in short, and historical, scientific, and textually linear thinking is being surpassed by a new, visionary, superficial mode of thinking. This is why we no longer see any sense in trying to distinguish between something illusionary and something nonillusionary, between fiction and reality. The abstract particle universe from which we are emerging has shown us that anything that is not illusory is not anything. This is why we must abandon such categories as true–false, real–artificial, or real–apparent in favor of such categories as concrete–abstract. The power to envision is the power of drawing the concrete out of the abstract.

Perception theory, ethics and aesthetics, and even our very sense of being alive are in crisis. We live in an illusory world of technical images, and we increasingly experience, recognize, evaluate, and act as a function of these images. We owe these images to a technology that came from scientific theories, theories that show us ineluctably that "in reality," everything is a swarm of points in a state of decay, a yawning emptiness. The science and the technology that developed from it, these triumphs of Western civilization, have, on one hand, eroded the objective world around us into nothingness and, on the other, bathed us in a world of illusion. And so it looks as though our historical development in the West has reached a final stage that does not look significantly different from a Buddhist worldview: a veil of Maya surrounds the yawning nothingness of nirvana. From this standpoint, the powerful stream of Western history is about to empty into the ocean of the timeless Orient.

There is considerable evidence that such a suicidal view of Western society is justified. And yet this view largely overlooks what is significant in the current cultural revolution. That is, the visionary power that we are beginning to use and that we owe to technical images makes us capable of calculating and computing the whirring nothingness around us. Therefore our illusions are not things we should abandon to fall into nirvana but rather are quite the opposite, our answer to the yawing nothingness that threatens us. The veil of technical images that surrounds us, as similar as it may appear to an Oriental veil, challenges us to an engagement neatly opposed to the Oriental. Our veil is not to be torn but rather woven more and more closely. The following chapters are dedicated to looking at this increasingly dense mesh.

that is what Schopenhauer's Veil of maya does too — it's phenomenologically too close, you can't tear it off

To Signify

The foregoing analysis of an emerging way of life was based on the hypothesis that we concentrate our attention more and more on our fingertips, a hypothesis that can be confirmed in the ubiquitous sight of the relevant gesture: pressing buttons. But fingertips don't just press, they also point toward something, mean something beyond themselves, indicate what they mean. I do not plan to delve into the problems bound up with such concepts as "point," "indicate," and "mean," for I am assuming that thanks to semiotics, *sign* and *meaning* have entered into common language and no longer need elucidation. The current interest in semiotics actually confirms a rising awareness of the role of fingertips in our new being-in-the-world. What I would like to do is ask a specific question: what do technical images indicate, to what do they point? And in the same context: what meaning do technical images have?

Stated so broadly, this question appears to allow for no reasonable answer. There are various kinds of technical images, and each kind seems to have a particular meaning. Photographs, for example, seem to mean scenes in the environment, films seem to mean events in the environment, and there seems no foreseeable limit to the potential meaning of computer-generated images. So the question posed earlier would have to be directed at each kind of technical image specially. And even within one kind of image, so many forms of meaning can be discerned that the question would have to be split up a second time. A photograph of a house, for example, appears to have a form of meaning completely different from a photograph of the sort incorrectly called "abstract." And so

41

the question of meaning would have to be posed specially to each technical image, and it would seem absurd to ask about the meaning of technical images in general. I will nevertheless attempt to show that technical images of any kind point in the same direction.

Before the arrival of electronically generated images, it appeared that all technical images arose through the capturing and holding of approaching particles or waves from the environment. For this reason, it seemed that they were depictions of an environment that was their meaning, each in its own way. In the context of synthetically generated images, this impression no longer holds up. They, too, in fact arise through the capturing and holding of approaching particles, but what they show, for example, an airplane that has yet to be built or a four-dimensional cube, cannot be seen as a depiction from the environment. As a result, the current tendency is to distinguish between two fundamentally different sorts of technical images: depictions and models. The one means what is and the other what could or should be. As soon as this distinction between depiction and model is made, problems arise. What do I actually mean when I say a photograph of a house depicts that house, and a computer image of an airplane yet to be built is a model? Do I perhaps mean that the house is somewhere out there, that is, real, and the airplane somewhere here inside and so only possible? Do I mean that the photographer discovered the house and the computer operator and invented the airplane? Or do I mean, somewhat more cleverly, that the house is the reason for the photograph (it was there before it was photographed, and the rays reflected from it caused the photograph) and the airplane is one possible result of the computer-generated image (the image was there first, and the airplane was made as a result of the image)? Any way I formulate the difference between depiction and model, I come to grief. For how does it look with the reality of photographically depicted house having been discovered or having caused the photograph? Doesn't the house actually look like what I see in the photograph (if there is any sense at all in asking how the house looks in reality)?

Hasn't the photographer discovered the house, like someone taking a walk and finding himself standing in front of a house (if there is any sense in distinguishing between discovery and invention in the first place)? And the house has not, after all, caused the photograph in the same sense that a dog's paw may be the cause of a track in the snow (if there is any sense in talking about causality in the particle universe). I won't maintain here that it's impossible to distinguish between the level of existence of a house there on the street and that of an airplane that is yet to be built. But I will maintain that it is impossible to distinguish between a representation and a model.

It can therefore be said of a photographer that he has made a model of a house in the same sense that the computer operator has made a model of a virtual airplane. And both models are, in different ways, representations of something, namely, sketches of calculated concepts that explain visualizations that in turn refer to the surrounding context. The photographer visualizes a house as houses seem to be in the outside, objective world. Then he takes an apparatus in hand to "grasp" (with concepts such as "perspective" or "shutter speed") what he has visualized. The apparatus calculates these concepts automatically, and the photographer presses a button to release the machine to carry out these calculations, making the vision of the house into an image. The computer operator visualizes an airplane as one might be found in the outside world. Then he takes an apparatus in hand (or reaches for an apparatus on his table) to "grasp" what he has visualized (through concepts such as "aerodynamic equations" or "production costs"). The apparatus calculates these concepts automatically, and the computer operator presses on the keyboard to make the apparatus carry out these calculations, making a visualization of an airplane appear on the screen. The same power to envision is at work in both cases, that of the photographer and of the computer operator, only it is more evident with the computer operator, who is more conscious than the photographer of this power. And so in considering technical images, it makes no sense to try to distinguish between representations and models. All technical images are visualizations.

The photographer of the house envisioned something, then, just as the computer operator did. In fact, he envisioned a house not as it actually is but as it should be. He invented rather than discovered the house. And the house is not the cause but the effect of his image, as we shall see. One can therefore say of the photographer that he produced a model of a house. On the other hand, one can also say of the computer operator that he made a depiction of an airplane. For like the photographer, he had an image and concept of what was to be shown, and that was what he depicted. The attempt to distinguish between depiction and model in the field of technical images is a lost cause, for no matter which form they take, they are not reproductive but productive images. The same visualizing power is at work in all of them.

This is not to say, however, that we must abandon all efforts to classify technical images according to their meaning. But other criteria must be chosen, criteria suited to the character of technical images. One can perhaps classify these images according to what level of information they contain: whether they are more or less informative, surprising, predictable images. I could say of a photograph of the cathedral in Florence, for example, that I had seen similar things many times before and that the image means almost nothing to me, and I may be able to say of a computerized image of a four-dimensional cube that I had seen nothing of the kind before and that the image was therefore meaningful; that is, I cannot distinguish between depictions and models, but I can distinguish redundant from informative images. Of course, I have not said what but only how the images mean—and that is the appropriate way to look at technical images.

It is customary to categorize technical images not according to their meaning but according to process, for example, as chemical or electronic images. Chemical images can be further divided into silent and still (photographs) and sounding and moving (films).

And electronic images can in turn be classified into various sub-categories—from video to computer images. Such a classification can be read chronologically: one technology follows another and can replace the previous one. If the first technical images were chemical (photographs) and the most recent electronic (synthesized images), then it is possible to confirm a general tendency for technical images, including and above all photographs, to become increasingly synthetic. Such a chronological reading of processes has undoubtedly affected systems organized according to meaning. For the technical process is itself informative, and the more recent it is, the more informative it is. From this standpoint, it is more surprising to see a synthetic image than it is to see a photograph. Photography is about to become redundant as a technology, and that is a challenge to photographers and filmmakers, for they judge images, as we've said, by the criteria redundant–informative, and they direct their visionary power toward producing informative images.

The question of what technical images mean is first and foremost a question of how the visualizing gesture is directed. Which way do the fingertips responsible for the images point? What is the maker's attitude? Where does he stand? To look at this position, this visualizing gesture with this question in mind is to realize that in it, a revolutionary new form of existence is finding expression, a powerful and violent reversal of human beings' attitude toward the world. This reversal is so powerful and violent that it is difficult for us to see. For envisioners, those who produce technical images, stand against the world, pointing toward it to make sense of it. Their gesture is a commanding, imperative gesture of codifying. Envisioners are people who raise themselves up against the world and point at it with their fingertips to inform it. Technical images have this imperative, codifying meaning. This is a reversal of human beings' former attitude toward the universe. Linear, historical consciousness, informed and produced through texts, inhabits a world that demands to be explained and interpreted, decoded. "Nature speaks." For such a consciousness, the world is a codified text, open to explanation and interpretation. The discourse of the sciences, explanations of processes in linear series is one result, among others, of the world challenging human beings in this way. Indicators, vectors of meaning run between the world and human beings; the world means something. Everything in the world is a sign of something, and a man must develop an attitude toward the world that permits him to decode this gigantic quantity of indications, signs, clues, for example, to derive so-called natural laws from the world. A man must bend over the world as over a text. *Adaequatio intellectus ad rem.*[1] Historical people take this stance, bending toward the world, bending consciousness toward the world.

As the world and consciousness dissolve into particles, this kind of attitude becomes impossible. The threads that organized processes into orderly rows have fallen apart, and so the world and consciousness have lost their textual character. Because the signs of the world are no longer organized into codes, there is nothing left in it to read, to decode. It is now clear that the signs of the world mean nothing, that they constitute an unstructured heap of elements. The structures historical consciousness read into these heaps were themselves produced in a textual way. The world has become meaningless, and consciousness will find nothing there but so many disconnected elements. We are, absurdly, in an absurd world. Bending toward the world is therefore an unsuitable stance and must be abandoned.

The disappointment we currently experience in every explanation, interpretation, and reading of the world (the discovery that there is nothing behind the world to be discovered) leads to a revolutionary new attitude toward the world. Disappointed, we stop bending, straighten ourselves up, and stretch out our arms against the world to point an index finger at it. From now on, all pointers, signs, traffic signals, and indicators point eccentrically away from us, and nothing more points toward us. From now on, we are the ones who project meaning on the world. And technical images are such projections. Whether they're photographs, films, videos, or computer images, all have the same meaning: to give absurdity a meaning.

The universe of traditional images consists of walls. These walls (whether cave walls or the walls of people's houses) are to be equipped with images that mirror the circumstances, for example, bulls or Emperor Franz Joseph. That is to say, the meaning of *bull* or *emperor* should be visible on the wall. And this is a deep, mysterious, sacred meaning. The pictures on the walls bring this meaning to the surface, they explain. The universe of technical images, by contrast, consists of no such tangible substrate (even though photographs may, for the time being, still be on paper, fixed to walls). This is about images projected into emptiness, into a field. And if these images show bulls or Emperor Franz Joseph, it will be to give meaning to this emptiness, this field in which we must live. Of course, bulls and emperors projected into nothingness in this way are no longer explanations but visualizations.

This reversal of attitude toward the world is as radical as the one in which our animal ancestors stood up and become hominids. At that time, however, we straightened up to reach into the world with our hands, to solve problems, to act. And now we straighten up to project vectors of meaning, to fabricate codes—that is to say, not to act, but to symbolize; not to inform objects, but to draft pure information. Technical images are such drafts, and the more they become electronic images, the purer they get.

The reversal of vectors of meaning has a disorienting effect on our inherited categories of meaning as we experience them in technical images for the first time. As long as the vectors pointed from the world toward us, the relevant question was, what is the meaning of the symbol I am to decode? For then there was something outside (the signified) that was represented by the symbol (the signifier). The symbol m means "mass" in the code of physics, and this "mass" is something outside, in the universe of physical discourse. A specific symbol means "house" in the code of traditional images, and this "house" is something out there in the universe of traditional images. After the reversal of the vectors of meaning, the question, what does it mean? has no position, for there is no outside. What does a technical image mean? is an incorrectly formulated question. Although they appear to do so, technical images don't depict anything; they project something. The signified of a technical image, whether it be a photograph of a house or a computer image of a virtual airplane, is something drawn from the inside toward the outside. And it is not out there until it has been drawn out. Therefore technical images must be decoded not from the signifier but from the signified, not from what they show but from what they show for. And the question appropriate to them is, to what end do technical images mean? To decode a technical image is not to decode what it shows but to read how it is programmed.

To make this inversion of interpretation, this reversal of our semantic categories, more comprehensible, let's compare technical with traditional images. Traditional images are mirrors. They capture the vectors of meaning that move from the world toward us, code them differently, and reflect them, recoded in this way, on a surface. Therefore it is correct to ask what they mean. Technical images are projections. They capture meaningless signs that come to us from the world (photons, electrons) and code them to give them a meaning. So it is incorrect to ask what they mean (unless one gave the meaningless answer: they mean photons). With them the question to ask is, what is the purpose of making the things they show mean what they do? For what they show is merely a function of their purpose.

What technical images show can be very similar to what traditional images show. A photograph of a house can look very similar to a painting of a house. And so it can appear that the photograph shows some particular house better than the painting does, as if the photograph were a better mirror of the house. But it is exactly the task of an inverted interpretation, a criticism suited to technical images, to show that this apparent "objectivity" of technical images is merely a function of the purpose their meaning serves. From the standpoint of so-called common sense, technical images are objective depictions of things out in the world. The critical project is to show that in defiance of common sense, they are not mirrors but projections that are programmed to make common sense appear mirrorlike.

Because technical images are projections, because they point one direction from the projector toward a horizon like, say, headlights and lighthouses, they must be decoded not as representations of things out in the world but as signposts directed outward. It is their projector, their program, that is the object of criticism. What technical images show depends on which direction they are pointing. That is to say, their significance is their meaning. In their case, the two coincide. The semantic and pragmatic dimensions of technical images are identical. To try to analyze what they show is to get lost in empty questions: Is the depicted house really out in the world, or is it just a surface? or Could the televised image of a politician be the performance of an actor imitating that figure? These are not good questions. They permit no answer relating to technical images because the questions assume a distinction between true and false, and in the universe of technical images, such distinctions have become superfluous. Technical images do not show us their meaning; they show us a way we may be directed. It is not what is shown in a technical image but rather the technical image itself that is the message. And it is a significant, commanding message.

We must criticize technical images on the basis of their program. We must start not from the tip of the vector of meaning but from the bow from which the arrow was shot. Criticism of technical images requires an analysis of their trajectory and an analysis of the intention behind it. And this intention lies in the link, the suture of the apparatus that produced them with the envisioners who produced them. Such a criticism requires new criteria, different from those for traditional images, criteria such as, say, information content or structural analysis. This is because technical images, with their inverted vectors of meaning, have an unprecedented meaning: they don't signify anything; they indicate a direction.

As they currently surround us, technical images signify models, instructions about the way society should experience, perceive, evaluate, and behave. They signify instructional programs. At present, envisioners and their apparatuses give their images not only a programmed but a programming significance. We currently live among commandingly outstretched index fingers, and we will blindly follow their instructions unless we realize that our blind following is exactly what they mean. Should we, in fact, realize this (and there are signs that we are beginning to do so), technical images could change their significance dramatically. They could then turn into dialogically constructed signposts, signposts in a world that has become absurd for those who have become aware of its absurdity.

To Interact

Technical images are not mirrors but projectors. They draw up plans on deceptive surfaces, and these plans are meant to become life plans for their recipients. People are supposed to arrange their lives in accordance with these designs. At least that is the way technical images function now, and this has given rise to a social structure in which people no longer group themselves according to problems but rather according to technical images. Such a social structure requires new social criteria, a new sociological approach. Classical sociology begins with people, their needs, desires, feelings, and knowledge, and divides society by relationships between people, for example, into groups such as families, nationalities, or classes. Classical sociology's cultural objects are mediations between people, and those objects—such as tables, houses, and autos—are therefore to be explained starting with the people. Such an approach and such criteria no longer apply to contemporary social structure. No longer people but rather technical images lie at the center, and accordingly, it is the relationships between technical images and people by which society must be classified, for example, by groups such as cinemagoers, television watchers, or computer users. Explanations for people's needs, wishes, feelings, and knowledge are to be found in technical images. For the sociology of the future, it means that people must be pushed out of the center toward the horizon of the field of inquiry, and this precisely to the extent the discipline seeks to preserve human freedom and dignity.

The relationship between technical images and people, the interactions between the two, are therefore the central issues of the coming cultural criticism, and all other issues are to be grasped from this point. What is immediately striking about this interaction is its intensely projective orientation. A technical image is directed toward a person. It presses in on him and finds him in even the most secret reaches of his private space. A person no longer goes from the private into the public, to the market, to school to inform himself, and if he does this in spite of the ubiquity of technical images, then this is because the new social structure has not yet fully asserted itself. Marketplace, school, and comparable public spaces are archaic spaces, unsuited to contemporary communication, and they will be abandoned. In fact, public announcements, demonstrations, and open-air festivals are still scheduled, and coaches drive about assembling tourists on beaches and ski trails. Yet this is not public, political assembly in the exact sense of the word but rather programmed disinformation. Technical images press through countless channels (television channels, picture magazines, computer terminals) into private space. They replace and improve the distribution of information that once occurred in public spaces and in so doing block off all public spaces. People don't go from the private into the public anymore because they can be better informed at home and because there is essentially no public space left to which to go.

One single technical image, namely, film, appears to run counter to the insistently projective orientation. In this case, it looks as if images are projected against a publicly erected screen and that people must go to a public space, the cinema, to see these images. It looks as though cinema is a kind of theater, namely, a "picture house." If this were true, one could claim that in film, a technical image makes a political gesture, drawing people from the private into the public. And if cinema were in fact a theater, that is to say, a place of visibility, of "theory," then one could say that film is a case of a technical image showing its viewer how to see through appearances and liberate himself from the image. Unfortunately, this is a mistaken view. Film is shown in cinemas not to awaken a political and philosophical consciousness in its viewers but because it relies on a technology from the nineteenth century, when receivers still needed to go to the sender. And since this technology no longer suits the general social structure, it is being improved. Films are being replaced by electronic recording technologies, and cinemas will disappear. There is a tendency to reconstitute cinema in new communicative contexts to preserve a political consciousness, a public space. Similar things have been undertaken in theater (at least since Brecht), in concerts (at least since Cage), and in the opera (at least since the site of the production was moved from the opera house to the street). But the question arises whether a political consciousness vegetating in an artificially preserved republic is worth the rescue effort.

The penetrating force of technical images drives their receiver into a corner, puts him under pressure, and this pressure leads him to press keys to make images appear in the corner. It is therefore an optimistic nonsense to claim to be free not to switch the television on, not to order any newspapers, and not to photograph. The energy required to withstand the penetrating force of technical images would project such a person out of the social context. Technical images do isolate those who receive them in corners, but they isolate those few who flee from them even further.

However, the reception of technical images does not end the communication process. Receivers are not sponges that simply absorb. On the contrary, they must react. On the outside, they must act in accordance with the technical images they have received: buy soap, go on holiday, vote for a political party. However, for the interaction between image and person under discussion here, it is crucial that receivers also react to the received image on the inside. They must feed it. A feedback loop must appear between the image and the receiver, making the images fatter and fatter. The images have feedback channels that run in the opposite direction from the distribution channels and that inform the senders about receivers' reactions, channels like market research, demography, and political elections. This feedback enables the images to change, to become better and better, and more like the receivers want them to be; that is, the images become more and more like the receivers want them to be so that the receivers can become more and more like the images want them to be. That is the interaction between image and person, in brief.

I will give two examples of this interaction, one of a film and the other of a television program. People sit in a darkened room and stare at a shimmering screen, on which giant forms appear to move. To sit there, they stood in line and then were distributed in geometrically ordered seats. An arithmetic row has become a geometric structure. Geometrically distributed, the people arrange themselves to receive the program (to be programmed) comfortably. From thinking objects, they have become geometrically extended objects. The Cartesian problem concerning the assimilation of the thinking subject to the extended object has been resolved in the cinema. Now the forms on the screen begin to jump instead of glide. The receivers know what it means: the projector is not working properly. If the receivers were slaves in a Platonic hell, they would welcome this, for it would be a step toward their release from looking at shadows. Cinemagoers, however, turn their heads toward the projector in irritation. They have paid to be betrayed. A consensus exists between them and the screen serving the interests of betrayal, a contract arising from feedback between the screen and the viewer. The contemporary cinemagoer is the result of having been fed by previous films, and the film on the screen is the result of having been fed by previous cinemagoers. The longer this mutual feeding continues, the stronger and more stable the consensus between image and people will become.

A Brazilian football club plays against a German one in Tokyo, and a Brazilian scientist watches this match on his television screen. He is among the few who want to escape technical images, and football is for him a means of alienation that he holds in contempt. Nevertheless, under the pressure of technical images, he has switched on his monitor and is entranced by the program. To dampen his enthusiasm, he calculates the length of the shadows the players throw and from the divergence between night and summer in Brazil and day and winter in Japan. He wants to dispel the magic (explain it scientifically) and so break the spell. He succumbs to the spell nevertheless, for the program activates layers of his personality he had thought long since buried (e.g., patriotism and rowdiness). At first, he thinks he has caught his enthusiasm from the enthusiasm of the Brazilian players. Under critical analysis, however, he confirms that these players were enthusiastic because they knew he and those like him were watching them. They were not playing as a function of the match but as a function of the image's transmission. They were engaged not (or not primarily) in the game but in television images. The enthusiasm is therefore an aspect of the feedback loop between image and people: the images become more exciting the more excited the receivers are, and the receivers that much more excited the more exciting the images are. And it happens even when they want to overcome the fascination of the images. The consensus between image and person, strengthened automatically through feedback, turns everyone into receivers, whether they were initially willing or not. And this consensus forms the core of a society governed by technical images.

A closed feedback circuit appears to have been set up between image and person. The image shows a washing machine that it wants us to buy, and we want the image to show us the washing machine because we want to buy it. The image shows a political party for which it wants us to vote, and we want the image to show us the party because we want to vote for it. This circuit can't actually be closed, however, for then the images would fall into entropic decay. They would always be the same images, reproduced ad infinitum. To get better (to always give the receiver something new, to be able to program innovatively), the image must get feedback from somewhere other than the receiver.

The images feed on history, on politics, science, art, on events of so-called daily life, and not only from current but also from past events. A photograph shows a political demonstration, a film a battle that has been fought this week, a television program a reconstruction of a nineteenth-century laboratory, a videotape a Renaissance building. In this way, it begins to look as though technical images were windows through which the receiver, having been driven into his corner, can observe things that are happening outside, and as if these images could always renew themselves because new things are always happening and because the sources on which they draw (past history) could never be exhausted. On closer inspection, however, both the windowlike character of technical images and the inexhaustibility of history oriented to past and future turn out to be in error.

Current events no longer roll toward some sort of future but toward technical images. Images are not windows; they are history's obstructions. The goal of the political demonstration is not to change the world but to be photographed. The goal of the battle that has been fought this week is to be filmed (the war in Lebanon was an important event, namely, the first in which this reversal of history away from the future and toward the image could be observed). And this initiates a novel sort of interaction, a feedback between image and event. The event dines on images, and the images dine on events. The moon landing was made to produce a television program, and a mission to the moon was on the television broadcasters' schedule. Part of getting married is to be photographed, and weddings conform to a photographic program. This will become increasingly clear for all events. Our historical consciousness defends itself against this new conception of history. We look for examples to establish that there are interactions free from the pull of technical images (e.g., the relatively image-free war in Afghanistan). We don't want to know about the threat to free exchange we see in these images. But it is just then that we realize to what extent an actual historical event such as that of the Afghani freedom fighters is being contained within the horizon of the present.

In its first, current phase, this reversal of events from the future to the image causes events to speed up. Events are caught in the undertow of the images and roll against them more and more wildly. One political event follows another more and more precipitously, a scientific theory is introduced, an artistic style replaces another almost before it has been established. The life span of a model is now measured not in centuries but in months. Progress accelerates. Yet the models don't fall over each other to change the world, but always, in theory eternally, to be shown in images. The linearity of history is turned against the circularity of technical images. History advances to be turned into images—posthistory.

That implies that the source from which history springs is beginning to dry up. This source is human freedom, that is, the decision to act to make the world the way it should be. But when one's actions are no longer directed toward the world but in the opposite direction, toward illusion, it is no longer possible to speak of freedom in the sense intended earlier. The one who acts then finds himself in a feedback relationship to the images very like the feedback relationship of the receiver. It can be seen in the example of the football game on television. Such an interaction is exciting for the receiver because the players are excited, and the players are excited because of the reception. History has become theater.

But on close inspection, past history also turns out to be a source that could be exhausted by technical images. It is true that we have assembled a huge quantity of information in the course of millennia. It is also true that a still greater quantity has been forgotten and could be recovered. But this quantity is still finite, and the gluttony of technical images is huge. Although the length of time images have been sucking up history is short compared to history's full duration, the first signs are appearing that this source is exhausted. Images are beginning to scratch at the bottom of a well thought to be bottomless. It makes no difference whether the images draw from the present or the past. For them, such historical categories have lost their meaning. For these images, the universe of history is nothing more than a field of possibilities from which images can be made. And once there is an image, everything is in the present and turns into an eternal repetition of the same, whether it is about a battle in the Lebanese War or in the Peloponnesian War. In this way, the images reach back to transform the past into a current program designed to program receivers, as the past is reduced to serving as a source of images.

What we call "history" is the way in which conditions can be recognized through linear texts. Texts produce history by projecting their own linear structure onto the particular situation. By imposing texts on a cultural object, one produces cultural history, and by imposing texts on natural objects (which happened relatively recently), one produces natural history. Such historicizing of conditions affects people's perspectives. Because nothing need repeat itself in a linear structure, each element has a unique position with respect to the whole. In this way, the historical way of reading the world turns each element into a unique occurrence, and each missed opportunity to shape the course of history becomes an opportunity definitively lost. This dramatizing state of mind characterizes historical consciousness. It stands in opposition to the prehistoric state of mind, for which everything in the environment (as in an image) must repeat itself, for which time moves in a circle, bringing everything back into its proper place, and for which the point is not to change the world but to escape just punishment for interfering with it. The wars between the Germans and the Romans offer an example of the collision between historical and prehistoric consciousness. They are part of Roman but not of German history because the Romans, but not the Germans, saw them as singular, unrepeatable events.

Technical images translate historical events into infinitely repeatable projections. Had there been videos at the time of the Battle of the Teutoburger Forest,[1] it would have been possible to spin this battle as new every evening, and had it been possible to synthesize images at the time, the battle could have been spun differently each evening. Someone who wants to make history today (to be a new Varus) has to contend with video. But that's ridiculous, for the new Varus would be aware that he only imagines an action, whereas the actual envisioner of the video image (even if that were he himself) acts according to completely unfamiliar criteria. A consciousness appropriate to technical images operates outside history. Stories and texts become materials for images. Technical images make Hermann just as impossible for the Cherusci, however. For Hermann felt powers (gods, fate) circling around him, whereas a new Hermann would know that his heroic deeds could be reprogrammed on video. For technical images, history and prehistory are pretexts from which to draw nourishment.

In their current first phase, technical images can still constantly renew themselves by feeding on history. But history is about to dry up, and this exactly because images are feeding on it, because they sit on historical threads like parasites, recoding them into circles. As soon as these circles are closed, the interaction between image and person will, in fact, become a closed feedback loop. Images will then always show the same thing, and people will always want to see the same thing. A cloak of endless, eternal boredom will spread itself over society. Society will succumb to entropy, and we can already confirm that the decay is on us: it expresses itself in the receivers' zeal for the sensational—there have always to be new images because all images have long since begun to get boring. The interaction between image and person is marked by entropy tending toward death.

memes today are recycled memes

Given the kind of interaction that currently exists between images and human beings, both with those who receive and those who act, we can expect an end to history with a probability bordering on certainty. No catastrophe of any sort (e.g., nuclear) is necessary—technical images are themselves the end. These images are programmed for an eternal return of the same; they were invented for this specific purpose: to bring an end to linearity, to reactivate the magic circle and a memory that eternally turns, bringing

(not in the way feminists had hoped; this is the nightmare edition

everything into the present. Not some series of catastrophes but rather technical images themselves are apocalyptic.

The current interaction between images and human beings will lead to a loss of historical consciousness in those who receive the images and, as a result, also to a loss of any historical action that could result from the reception of the image. But this current interaction is not yet leading to the development of a new consciousness, unless it changes radically, unless the feedback is interrupted and images begin to mediate between people. Such a rupture of the magical circle between image and person is the task we face, and this rupture is not only technically but above all existentially possible. For images are beginning to bore us, in spite of the contract we have with them. The traffic between images and people is the central problem of a society ruled by technical images. It is the point where the rising so-called information society may be restructured and made humane.

To Scatter

Technical images are at the center of society. But because they are so penetrating, people don't crowd around them; rather they draw back, each into his corner. A technical image radiates, and at the tip of each ray sits a receiver, on his own. In this way, technical images disperse society into corners. Each technical image (except for film, as discussed) is received as the end point of a ray, as a "terminal." So the scattered society forms no amorphous heaps; rather the corners are distributed according to a structure that radiates outward from the center. These rays (channels, media) structure the society as a magnet structures iron filings. The society, spread apart by the magnetic fascination of technical images, is indeed structured, and an analysis of the media can bring this structure to light. Media form bundles that radiate from the centers, the senders. *Bundles* in Latin is *fasces*. The structure of a society governed by technical images is therefore fascist, not for any ideological reason but for technical reasons. As technical images presently function, they lead on their own to a fascistic society.

behavior becomes ideology

This social structure began to appear only a few decades ago, breaking through the previous social structures like a submarine through ice. As it breaks through, social groups that bound human interaction fall apart. Families, nationalities, classes disintegrate. Sociologists and cultural critics are characteristically more interested in the fall of the earlier social structure than they are in the rise of the new. They pay more attention to the cracking ice than to the rising boat. This is the reason they speak of a decaying society rather than a new society. They criticize the falling structures rather than criticizing the new ones. With the family, they speak of phallocratic machismo; with nationality, of chauvinism; with class, of the struggle between classes. They are kicking dead horses.

The explanation for this critical blind spot is easy to find. Disintegrating social forms are more interesting than new ones because they are sanctified by familiarity. The family, for example, is a serious matter, and a high value is placed on the human relationships that constitute it (e.g., the love between man and woman or between parents and children). When families fall apart, the underlying values are lost. Therefore a constructive critique of the decaying family (e.g., the suggestion of alternative family models such as kibitzes or cooperatives) appears to be justifiable. But in fact, every attempt to rescue the family from the intrusion of television or the computer is a hopeless, reactionary project. It is one of the ice shards that drift and dissolve.

In comparison to the family, new social forms, such as newspaper subscribers, are not interesting. They are not sanctified. There is no higher value ascribed to the relationship between the newspaper, its sender, and its receivers. Those who criticize these new social forms appear to be sidetracked, but in fact, it is exactly these new forms that demand our concentrated attention. For not only are they displacing the old, sanctified forms, they are also consecrating new relationships and new values. If the point of cultural criticism is to maintain and increase human freedom and dignity, then its focus must be on just these new forms. For only if we can recognize the rising fascistic patterns in time to change them may we hope that a humane society could emerge from technical images' revolt against our inherited social structure.

The present cultural revolution is technical, not ideological. Therefore inherited political categories such as "liberal" and "socialist," "conservative" and "progressive," no longer apply. That may confound critics. But really effective revolutions have always been technical. Let us take as an example the most powerful revolution known to us, that of the Neolithic. It grew out of the new technologies of farming and animal husbandry. These technologies overturned the earlier Mesolithic structures and led to new family groups, to the village, to war, to private ownership, to slavery. These new social forms were sanctified after the fact and endowed with value. Not the founders of Neolithic religions but the inventors of cows and flour were the revolutionaries, and had a contemporary critic tried to evaluate the situation from the standpoint of outmoded ideologies (e.g., had he tried to evaluate the hunter's value), he would have missed the point. The first Industrial Revolution may be another case in point. It, too, was technical. Its revolutionaries were the inventors of machines, and the social forms they produced (e.g., the proletariat) were consecrated only in retrospect by religious figures such as Marx or Lenin.

Today's revolutionaries are not Kaddaffis or Meinhofs but rather the inventors of technical images. Niépce, Lumière, the number-less and nameless inventors of computer technology, these are the ones who have brought the new social forms about. And so if we want to instigate a humane society, we must understand the new technologies, not higher values. For example, we must ask whether it is technically possible to modify the fascistic structure of radiating images. Such technical questions are the politically interesting ones today. We can leave the retroactive consecration and valorization for a later time and someone who founds religions. Those who think politically according to older categories and perhaps think that technology is politically neutral are missing the cultural revolution.

The destruction of traditional social groups through technical images (e.g., the family through television or nationality through satellites) looks like decadence from the standpoint of the past. Society drifts into corners, into the "lonely mass," and interpersonal bonds, the social tissue, dissolve. The young Californians who sit in isolation at their computer terminals with their backs to one another have no social awareness. They belong to no family and identify with neither nationality nor class. From a nonideological, that is, phenomenological perspective, it is possible to recognize the appearance of the new social connective tissue. It is possible to recognize the threads that bind these new people to the senders of technical images. It becomes clear that we are dealing not with an asocial person but with one who is very profoundly socialized, although in a new sense. In fact, we are dealing with people who are so completely socialized that we justifiably fear for their individuality, despite their apparent isolation. The scattering into isolation appears here as the flip side of the coin *Gleichschaltung* (political alignment).[1]

According to the current circuitry for technical images, this fear is justified. But there are signs that this pattern could change. For the new social structure is dynamic. The threads that order it run from image to isolated person and back to image. This traffic between image and person, this feedback that threatens to become entropic, forms the isolating, homogenizing core of society. But there are threads that start to run another direction, namely, from one person to another, straight across the bundles of rays that bind images to people, dialogic threads that cross the horizontal, discursive media bundles. Dialogic threads (such as cable, videophones, or conferencing video) could open the fascist tissue of the rising society to the kind of web we are in the habit of calling "democratic." And if such a web was actually constructed and images installed according to such a pattern, one could no longer speak of isolation and political coordination. For then people of the future would truly be in dialogue, in a global conversation.

Whether and how dialogic threads can be drawn is a technical question. But the truly revolutionary engagement would be to turn this technical question into a political one, and that means to turn the scattering of the population to the service of human freedom and dignity by rebuilding the circuitry of the images, directing the force of the rising society toward the advancement these values. Such an engagement assumes, of course, that the rebuilding of the circuitry itself be undertaken dialogically. For when the dialogic threads from senders, such as governments or commercial institutions, are introduced at present, they must remain in the service of the sender, despite their dialogic function. In this way, the net preserves its fascistic, bundled structure. To turn a technical question into a political one, it must be torn from the technician's hands. Technology has become too serious a matter to be left to technicians. In other words, the revolutionary reconstruction of the current circuitry of technical images into a dialogical, democratic one presumes that a general consensus must exist in this respect. The people must want it.

There is no prospect for such a consensus, however. On the contrary: at present, there is a consensus between the images and their bundled streams, on one hand, and the receivers, on the other. The people want to be scattered by the images so that they don't have to collect and assemble themselves, as they would if there were in fact a dialogue. They are happy not to have to do it anymore. For at one time, when society was ordered by interpersonal relationships, there was an out-group and an in-group, there was public space outside (e.g., outside the family) and a private space inside, and one spread himself out in public to assemble himself in private. Hegel called this the "unhappy consciousness": if I go out into the world, I lose myself in it, and if I go into myself to collect myself, then I am lost to the world. This unhappy consciousness is happily no longer required. For in the dispersed society, there is neither inside nor outside. The unhappy consciousness rests. There you can spread out as you wish, and every dialogue is dangerous because it could awaken the unhappy consciousness from its sleep. The consensus between image and person rests on the disinclination of people to collect themselves, as much as on the intention of the images to disperse people.

But unhappy consciousness is the only form of consciousness there is, for happiness is not conscious. People want to disperse themselves to lose consciousness, to become happy. The present dispersal of society has resulted from a general wish to be happy:

we are on the way to a happy society. Shangri La is just around the corner. Everyone is at once a mouth that sucks on the images and an anus that gives the undigested, sucked thing back to the images. Psychoanalysis describes this happiness as the oral–anal phase; cultural analysis calls this happiness "mass culture." It is happiness at the level of the nursery, intellectually as well as morally and aesthetically. The present dispersal of society can be seen as a move toward this happy twilight condition.

Today's revolutionaries, those who want to spin threads through the narcotizing discourse, decline to take part in this general consensus about happiness. They are muckrakers. They want to awaken this fading consciousness because they believe that the mindless happiness sponsored by the images is demeaning; that is, present-day revolutionaries are working toward something that only they want. They take action exactly against the general consensus between images and people, and they know they can achieve nothing as long as the others don't go along. They know that it isn't technically difficult to draw dialogic threads, such as cables, video telephones, or video circuits, but that such circuits are merely gadgets and will remain nonsensical as long as there is no political will to use them to rebuild the society, as, for example, the current pornographic babble with Minitel in Strassbourg.[2] Present-day revolutionaries know that they first have to build a consensus. Their action is not against images but against the current feedback consensus between images and people.

This action is utterly unspectacular, for if it were spectacular (visible in images), it would be self-defeating. It would then simply assist in dispersing people. The people that are shouting and sounding alarms today, the Che Guevaras and Khomeinis, and those who count as revolutionaries are really entertainers. They are spectacular, and the spectacle they present assists the images in dispersing us more and more effectively. The true revolutionaries, on the other hand, do not appear in the images. But that does not necessarily mean that they are inaccessible to the scattered society.

It is true that they can't be seen in the images, but we can see them by looking through the images. For although the revolutionaries don't show themselves in the images, they appear in the manner in which the images show themselves. Revolutionaries can manipulate the images so that people begin to glimpse the possibility of using these images to initiate previously unimaginable interpersonal relationships, that the images could be used for dialogue, the exchange of information, and the fabrication of new information. Because the scattering images are beginning to bore people, and a dialogical game through images with other people could be suspenseful and exciting, one can just about imagine that the revolutionaries could succeed in breaking the feedback loop between image and person and creating a new dialogical consensus.

Contemporary revolutionaries are not actively opposed to the images themselves but rather to the integrated circuitry. They actively promote dialogical, rewired images. Contemporary revolutionaries are envisioners (photographers, filmmakers, video makers, computer programmers) grounded in the revolution in technical images. Their visionary powers are focused on a society in which people exchange information through images and, in so doing, constantly produce new information, improbable situations. Only as a result of this new capacity to visualize does it become possible to conceive of such a social formation. The revolutionaries want to change not only the underlying structure but the surface of the so-called information society. Soa Steve Jobs?

The social structure that is now appearing represents a synchronization of radiating images with the dispersed, lonely, depersonalized people who sit at the terminals of these rays. Revolutionary visualization tries to replace this structure with another in such a way that the images bring new interpersonal relationships into being and lead to new social configurations, the names of which remain unknown for now. Such a social configuration would still be characterized by technical images. In fact, it would deserve to be called an "image culture" more than our current culture does.

But instead of the traffic between people and images, it would be traffic between people by way of images that would lie at the heart of such a society. And only then would the media earn the name that unjustly designates them today. For only then would they link person to person, a bit like nervous pathways and nerve cells join together. On the basis of such links, the society would continually produce new information. Such a society would perhaps best be called a "global brain." It would be a humane society, for to generate, transmit, and store information is uniquely human. This, I believe, is the project of the new revolutionaries.

It is an opposition to the present society, controlled as it is by discursively ordered images. But it is not an attempt to reconstruct any social configuration from the past. Contemporary dispersal cannot be reversed. On the contrary, it requires a new form of assembly. It is high time that our received, consecrated groups fell apart. They were pernicious, ideologically grounded, misery-making groups. Now that they are about to disintegrate completely, new groups can be formed. They can be "informed." The task is to reintegrate a society that has disintegrated into the infinitesimal. Such formulations of contemporary activism are intended to show how firmly contemporary revolutionaries are rooted in the dimensionless universe, on the grounds of hallucinatory, image-producing abstractions.

Technical images must first destroy the old society so that a new one may appear. Today we are witnessing, not decadence, but the emergence of a new social form. And we can actually see this now. The relationship between people and images is descending into entropy, a fatal boredom is setting in, generating an impulse toward a new consensus opposed to mass culture and in favor of a humane visual culture. This new social structure can be seen, with a bit of optimism, as a transitional phase in the rise of a new culture.

To Instruct

Technical images are currently connected so that their senders are at the center of society, places from which the images are broadcast to scatter and disperse the society. They are precarious places. When you approach them, whether to take part (to join in the broadcasting) or to criticize (to remodel the circuitry), they present themselves as illusions. They are like the proverbial onion: layer after layer comes away, but when everything has been understood, explained, there's nothing left. It appears that no one and nothing lies at the center of contemporary society: senders are nothing but those dimensionless points from which the media bundles stream. *death of the sender*

For cultural criticism, this is an unpleasant discovery. When you're criticizing culture to change it, you want to be fighting something solid (e.g., dark men behind the scenes or gray eminences with evil intentions that can be exposed). If you start to expose contemporary society, however, you realize that there is nothing and no one to fight. One is not so much tilting at windmills as storming Kafka's castle. For one is fighting a how rather than a what. Not people and things, but contents. Not images and the human interests that stand behind them, but circuitry. Therefore it is not surprising that many cultural critics yield to these new demands and, all evidence to the contrary, go on looking for manipulators and power brokers among the senders.

They immerse themselves in the senders. These are soft, padded places, areas of software, where such immersion is possible. What they find is that apparatuses and the functionaries that sit before them are becoming more and more numerous, smaller, more completely automatic and faster. A button pressing is under way, a noise that is becoming steadily quieter. The critics confirm that each time a button is pressed, an order goes to some medium to send out an image. They have the impression of having stumbled into the center of contemporary decision making, and this in a double sense of "decision." First, the senders appear to subjugate the society by attracting a higher and higher proportion of the people, turning them into functionaries. Second, the senders appear to use their buttons to prescribe what happens to the society, what it is to do. This impression is mistaken because under current conditions, the concept "decision" demands rethinking, as will be shown in a later chapter.

It is true that more and more people serve the senders, the apparatus. Work in the traditional sense, namely, the gesture that alters the form of our surroundings, can be turned over to automated apparatuses more and more effectively in more and more workplaces. Therefore it is true even now that most of us no longer work and that, in the foreseeable future, all of us will be without work—unemployed. We will be "free," that is, to press buttons, if only to program the machines to do the work—and so to enter fully into the service of the sender (the service sector).

But this does not mean, as many cultural critics assume, that instead of farmers, the proletariat, and the middle class, we now have a new class before us, namely, functionaries, and that we can proceed with roughly the same categories as before. Functionaries are not a social class. What characterizes a class is class consciousness, an ideology drawing on work experiences, work knowledge, and work values. Class is a way of life. But being a functionary is not a way of life, and so there is no functionary ideology, no functionary class consciousness. For a function takes up only a steadily diminishing amount of time, and the experiences, knowledge, and values of functionaries do not derive from this time but from images seen at leisure. What is crucial for contemporary society is not that we are becoming functionaries for senders but that we are receivers. Our way of life, our ideology, is not that of functionaries but that of receivers. Senders control us not because we serve them but because they serve us.

It is equally true that each press of a button sends commands to the media and through the media to society. But it is an error to see this as a gesture of decision making. Button-pressing functionaries (typists, photographers, bank directors, generals, presidents of the United States—in short, those who compute) do choose among the keys available to them, but this choice is prescribed for them. And this is not done by anyone or anything but by the automated self-feeding structure of the broadcast program. For example, the American president presses a button according to a program: a video image appears as programmed on his terminal, and this image shows Russian missiles over Alaska. He presses another button according to the program, and cities fall, as programmed, to ashes.

Of course, not all button pressing has equally significant consequences, and so it can be ordered hierarchically. In such a hierarchy, the American president would stand above the bank director because the president's button pressing transforms cities into ashes, and the touch of the bank director's only sets industries into competition. The bank director would rank higher than the television operator because when the operator presses, he only calls up images on terminals. But such a hierarchy can't be maintained. For when the president presses a button, cities are destroyed as a result of the video operator having pressed one. And if he, too, is pressing as a result of the Russian general secretary having pressed a button, then the general secretary's action has, from his standpoint, triggered the action of the video operator. It is therefore an error to see functionaries, however highly they may be placed, as power brokers or decision makers or to suspect more highly placed, concealed decision-making centers behind them. It happens automatically. With respect to the sender, there is no elite for us either to embrace or reject.

[handwritten marginal note:] the button press exist the decision

[handwritten note at bottom:] → but who is winning from this? who is making the money?

Functionaries themselves do tend to misrepresent the situation when asked (or even without being asked), however. Not long ago, for example, the French president said on television that the "strike force" was only an inactive tool that was entirely at his disposal. The president's illusion of being Louis XIV (*l'Etat, c'est moi*) would be touching if it did not bode so ill for any understanding of the current situation. We are disposed to lend the functionaries credence. If they claim to control the apparatus, aren't they supposed to know what they're saying? Regrettably, they do not know what they're saying. They, too, are carried off by the languid, automatic flow of the apparatus. They are blind to it. This is why, if we want to look into it, we must ask generalists, people with an overview of the state of the apparatus. This investigation shows that it doesn't matter whether the French president is Mitterrand, Giscard, or Dupont. He will press the red button at the moment prescribed by the program of the apparatus.

Social centers, senders, are padding, whereas apparatuses and functionaries calculate and compute instructions as instructed. Acknowledging this embarrassing but unavoidable fact obliges us to ask two questions: how did it come to this? and what can be done about it? Both questions were implicit in the previous chapters and will now be considered explicitly.

Around the mid-nineteenth century, as the guiding principles that had once ordered the world and structured thinking in a linear way began to disintegrate, the problem of how to reintegrate the dispersed particles made its appearance. This problem had already been solved in the seventeenth century in a partially satisfying way in the field of mathematics. Newton and Leibniz invented calculus, and this method was then applied, on one hand, to the physical universe and, on the other, to logic. At this point, apparatuses had to be produced to put this method into practice: first, apparatuses whose purpose was to integrate the world's particle elements—the camera was the first of these apparatuses—and later, apparatuses whose purpose was to integrate the particle elements of thought, leading to the computer. Such apparatuses, in contrast to earlier machines, do not operate in a procedural continuum but in a Democritan[1] universe of particles that they must capture.

As soon as such machines went into production, something like a revolutionary discovery came to light, namely, that atoms combine with one another spontaneously and that, eventually, all such combinations must occur spontaneously. The discovery was subversive because it led to automation. However, if one reads Democritus in light of this discovery, one is surprised to realize that he already had the basic idea of automation. His concept of *klinamen* (the accidental deviation of a particle from its prescribed path) can be read as a preview of mechanical automation. At this point, it became clear that it was not necessary to capture the particle elements: they do this spontaneously. What is necessary is that two other conditions are met. First, one must know which of the available combinations one wants to produce. It is true that all combinations are foreseeable in principle, but some are more probable than others. It was the improbable combinations (the informative ones) that were wanted, and they only occur by blind chance after very lengthy—astronomically lengthy—computation. So, second, the play of pure chance had to be accelerated to secure the desired combinations within a human time frame. This, then, is automation: to build an apparatus that speeds up chance events and to prescribe (program) it to stop when the desired coincidence has occurred.

Looking more closely, it becomes clear how revolutionary automation is. For from now on, human freedom no longer consists in being able to shape the world to one's own desires (apparatuses do this better) but to instruct (program) the apparatus as to the desired form and to stop (control) it when this form has been produced. Here a new freedom arises, which apparatuses are supposed to serve. But unfortunately, the exact opposite very soon began to occur. Apparatuses become faster and faster and slipped out of control. The number of automatically produced coincidences and their consequences surpass any human capacity to control them. In this way, the possibility of stopping the apparatus at the desired coincidence is lost. The program becomes independent of human intention. It becomes autonomous and rolls on until every coincidence has been realized, even those human beings originally wanted explicitly to avoid. Examples of such autonomy of programs can be seen everywhere—not only in the military but also in the political, industrial, cultural, and administrative apparatuses. The original intention of producing the apparatus, namely, to serve the interests of freedom, has turned on itself. Certainly for the time being, most apparatuses are not so completely automatic that they can get along without human intervention. They need functionaries. In this way, the original terms *human* and *apparatus* are reversed, and human beings operate as a function of the apparatus. A man gives an apparatus instructions that the apparatus has instructed him to give. In this way, a powerful flood of programs is unleashed, a flood of software with which people no longer pursue any particular intention but rather use to issue instructions as a function of an earlier program. As these programs become more complex and clever, they demand faster, smaller, and cheaper apparatuses, more congenial hardware. And so one generation of apparatuses after another appears. With each new generation, human intention recedes further into the background—the intention, that is, that produced the first generation of apparatuses.

For the time being, in the current generation of apparatuses, this original human intention has not yet completely disappeared. The evidence for this is that a given program cannot be run on all apparatuses. The variability of programs is one last echo of the original intention. For example, it looks as though two giant apparatuses, the American and the Soviet, are fighting one another over our heads and that the difference between them could be traced back to an original human intention. But such a polytheistic view of the situation (Zeus fights Pluto, and we have to choose between the two, despite having surrendered to them) does not apply. Human beings, in fact, originally programmed these two apparatuses, but they have become largely autonomous. They are neither gods nor supermen but subhuman, obdurate automata. They roll along blindly, according to accelerated chance. They could destroy one another (and the humanity that feeds on them) by chance, but that is just one of the possible coincidences that lie in their program. Another coincidence is more probable: as the two apparatuses roll along, they interact with one another, mesh, and move randomly toward a complete synchronization of their two programs to a global totalitarianism of apparatuses. And between these two possibilities, there are other possible, theoretically calculable, futurizable possibilities.

The evidence can already be seen everywhere that a full synchronization of the two (and of all) programs is the most probable alternative. The tendency toward a global unification and coordination of all programs to a global metaprogram can be seen in a mass culture that takes the same form all over the world. Clothing, dance, music, and above all images hardly look any different in America than they do in Russia, Brazil, or the Philippines, and that despite all the differences that could still be established between the apparatuses that operate in those places.

At present, the individual senders have not become standardized with respect to one another but still send out bundles that partially cross one another. Around these transmission points sit functionaries who press the keys of apparatuses, especially those that compute images. For these images model the behavior, perception, and experience of all other functionaries. The functionaries instruct the images about how the images should instruct the receivers. The apparatuses instruct the functionaries how they are to instruct the images. And other apparatuses instruct these apparatuses about how the functionaries are to instruct. Throughout this seeming and self-obscuring hierarchy of instruction, one senses a general entropic tendency toward a global metaprogram, and no one and nothing other than this implacable self-determination is behind it all.

This implacable self-determination, this tendency toward entropy, probably indicates the way we are going: toward a global totalitarian apparatus. But it is human to oppose entropy. This is why humans produced the apparatus in the first place: to produce improbable situations. They lost control of the apparatus, and now it produces the probable automatically. And so the question is, can they regain control and so achieve the opposite of the probable, the opposite of a totalitarian apparatus? As independent beings, scattered and isolated functionaries and receivers, people have definitively lost control of the apparatus, as this chapter tried to show. The apparatuses' capacities, the speed at which they can compute, their storage capacity, their memory, is greater than the capacity of the human brain. On the other hand, the capacity of society as a whole, as a collective brain, is in all probability still greater than the capacity of all the apparatuses put together.

Apparatuses are, in fact, exceptionally fast idiots that forget nothing, but they are idiots nevertheless. Therefore, although individual receivers and functionaries cannot take control of the apparatus, the society as a whole could. This is what the "unspectacular new revolutionaries" are trying to do.

Society as a whole should program the apparatus as a whole to produce automatically improbable situations and to stop at desirable situations. To do this, society must reconstruct the circuitry of the sender to stop functioning and receiving and instead to program and constantly reprogram the broadcasts. Such a reconstruction is technically possible by means of telematics, which could support a worldwide dialogue about the apparatus. It allows for a broad, worldwide consensus relating to the programming of apparatuses to be reached cybernetically. Technically, the apparatus allows itself to be bent to serve the society. Technically, it could be made to serve a democratic function. But the reconstruction of the circuitry of the sender is not solely a technical but also a political question. First, an agreement must be reached to remodel the senders so that they may serve a future consensus. This consensus to produce a consensus is what today's engaged envisioners—all the photographers, film people, video people, computer people—are trying to bring about. By reconstructing the role of images in society, they want to bring about a general reconstruction of all broadcasting. Then the global totalitarian apparatus could be avoided, and instruction would be directed dialogically against the apparatus—in other words, not programmed democracy but democratic programming. Only this must happen rather quickly, or the capacities of the apparatuses as a whole will surpass the capacities of the society as a whole.

where are we now?

To Discuss

The technology that would enable the current discursive circuitry of technical images to be reconfigured into dialogical circuitry is called "telematics." This name is new, an amalgam of *telecommunication* and *informatics,* but the principle to which the new name refers is far older, in fact, just as old as the technology of calculating and computing particle elements, a product of the first half of the nineteenth century. Yet the name's novelty is itself significant for understanding the current situation. For it shows that we have only very recently become aware of the principle of calculating and computing, that we have only recently realized that the same principle applies to both communication through the radiant streaming of particle elements (telecommunication) and the grasping of particle elements as new information (the production of technical images). And only since this has been recognized can technical images really begin to expose their inherent properties. We have been consciously experiencing the revolution of technical images for only a few years.

In retrospect, this delayed awakening is surprising. It is surprising that the inventers of the first apparatuses, namely, of photographic and telegraphic apparatuses, did not recognize that both were constructed according to the same principle and so could be linked. Both photography and telegraphy rely on the programming of particle elements that they encode, the camera on a two-dimensional pictorial code and the telegraph on a linear Morse code. So both overturn the historical categories associated with space evolving in time and, with them, a social structure of groups spatially and temporally separated from one another. Both photography and telegraphy produce new social structures in which everyone, everywhere, is at the same time. By storing everything in a memory that is permanent and infinitely reproducible, fully accessible to all, photography renders and keeps everything present. Thanks to the telegraph, information is instantly accessible everywhere. And yet it didn't occur to anyone at the time that photographs could be telegraphed.

Of course, it is possible to explain this initial oversight. One might say that photographs were coarse, that they were chemical, and so not compatible with the fine electromagnetic structure of the telegraph, that photographs had first to become electromagnetic to be transmitted telegraphically. But these technical explanations are insufficient. It is more probable that telegraphy was initially regarded as a new sort of writing and so did not appear to be constructed, exactly like a photograph, out of particles. Two separate developments arose from this misunderstanding: from the telegraph came the telephone and all the other dialogic telecommunications, and from the photograph came film and all the other technical images. And now it becomes clear that these two developments are fundamentally the same and that technical images are inherently suited to the forms of transmission used in telecommunications, that technical images are inherently dialogical.

The convergence of images and telecommunications is so new that we experience it as a technical phenomenon and not yet as a cultural one. This is why we speak of things like lasers, cables, satellites, digital transmission, and computer language as if only technicians should speak of such things. But that is a temporary setback. The apparatuses will become more and more user friendly, and in the foreseeable future, every child will be able to play (dialogue) with any other child, just as every child can now take a picture with no idea about photographic technique. To receive, synthesize, and transmit technical images will, in short, turn into a programmed gesture of key pressing. Therefore it is a fundamental misunderstanding to suppose that some prior technical knowledge is a condition of combining images with telecommunications. On the contrary: any such prior knowledge must be bracketed out to grasp the cultural and existential impact of telematics.

This can be seen clearly by observing telematic gadgets as they are currently manufactured—for example, at the exhibition Electra that was organized in Paris recently. There one could see people synthesizing images on computers, storing them in memory, and transmitting them to others in dialogue. The result is a game of program permutation, that is, empty chatter. In evidence here is a form of distraction at the intellectual, political, and aesthetic level of the nursery. People press their dialogical keys according to a program prescribed by senders. The exhibition organizers (senders) insist that the exhibition is intended to introduce people to telematic technology. It is meant to be a kind of elementary school for telematics, and so the low level is to be expected. But in fact, with this and nearly every other instance of telematic gadgets today, this is the sender's way of subordinating the dialogical function of technical images to the command discourse of the sender, to make dialogical nets support discursively bundled transmissions. The strategy is generated automatically. The sender functions in such a way as to make the dialogic threads "spontaneously" strengthen and solidify discursive bundles.

And so it is difficult to recognize the revolutionary potential of telematics, its capacity to tear discursive bundles apart. From looking at telematic gadgets, it is not immediately clear what sleeps within, for example, that discursive newspapers delivered to the door could be replaced by video disks to which we could respond, or that instead of writing letters, we could exchange experiences, thoughts, and feelings with one another in the form of images. Instead of going into town, we could shop and take care of legal and political business such as voting from a terminal at home. In short, it is not immediately obvious that telematics, even in its current form, is technically capable of rendering superfluous such things as newspapers, books, letters, businesses, offices, factories, theaters, cinemas, concert halls, and exhibitions but also such things as the postal service, radio and television, or money. In other words, it is not immediately obvious that telematics, even in its present, underdeveloped form, has the potential to overthrow all current discursive as well as dialogic social structures.

We have probably never been so incapable of predicting the immediate future. Every revolution has paralyzed its victims and rendered them blind, for example, the aristocracy in the French Revolution or the Jews under Nazism. But the telematic revolution affects the whole society, not just part of it. And so even those who have set it in motion can't see where it's going. It is not from fear that we close our eyes to the immediate future; rather we do so because we can't confront the triumph of the images that flood over us and that we ourselves now partly produce. This triumph doesn't frighten us; on the contrary, it awakens a feeling of emptiness. Obviously we're happy that things like work, politics, and art (in short, history in the traditional sense) have no future. We are happy to get rid of all those things that restrict us. But what will be left? Everyone all over the world will shortly be accessible to us; we'll be playing chess with someone in the Antipodes and spending an amusing evening with geographically scattered friends around an electronic round table. Only, what will we talk about with these people, when we all have the same, centrally programmed information? When we are served by the same central memory? And when we are so neutralized that even as our interests appear to conflict, the conflict has been fed into us from the central memory? Even our arguments are empty chatter (e.g., as can be seen in pseudo-dialogue such as parliamentary debates or so-called negotiations between employers and unions). The telematically drawn, dialogic threads will carry no conversations but only empty chatter. And the more they may seem to bring us together, the more they will disperse us into isolated individuals who have nothing to say to one another. They will grind those human bonds such as love and friendship, but also hate and antagonism, down into empty chatter. And although the threads appear to be dialogic, they will in fact make all dialogue superfluous, redundant—hence the feeling of emptiness.

Before I attempt to show that it is a mistake to close one's eyes to the telematic revolution, that it contains possibilities for real dialogue of unprecedented richness, I must discuss the relationship between discourse and dialogue in general.

From the standpoint of communication, every social structure is characterized by a collaboration between discourse and dialogue. For from this point of view, society is a web whose function is to produce and transmit information so that it can be stored in memory. Discourse is the method through which information is transmitted and dialogue the method through which it is produced. Because this essay is to be an investigation of the dialogic use of images, among other things, I will have something to say about the dialogic production of information in the following chapters.

Using such communicological[1] criteria, societies can be classified into three types. The first type is the ideal society, in which discourse and dialogue are in balance. Dialogue nourishes discourse, and discourse provokes dialogue. The second type is the dialogic society. The Enlightenment presents an example. There are a great many dialogic circles producing an increasing quantity of information—scientific, political, and artistic. But because these elite circles have no means of passing the information on, the society threatens to fall apart into an informed elite and an uninformed mass. The third type is the discursive society. The late medieval period offers an example of it: the centrally radiating discourse of the Church controls the society, the sources of information threaten to dry up from an absence of dialogue, and the society is threatened with entropy.

The medieval–Catholic characteristics of the present time become recognizable if one applies this model. Centrally radiating discourses dominate us, too, and society is threatened with entropy.

The telematic dialogues that are technically possible now appear as a variant of medieval disputation. They revolve around the radiating programs. And should they nevertheless lead to new information, it will now be disregarded as noise, whereas at that time, it was heresy, rendered ineffective through anathema. Such a comparison of the present with the Catholic Middle Ages also allows us to recognize differences. The crucial difference is the authoritative character of discourse of that time and the automatic character of discourse in the present. The Church was not an apparatus; rather it had an author, Jesus, and authorities, priests. The dialogues of that time were authoritative discussions—between priests. Today apparatuses program discourse automatically; this can be seen by the absence of any author or authority. Telematic dialogues today carry neither authority nor responsibility. At that time, unwanted information that may have been generated through dialogue, for example, in the so-called dispute on universals,[2] was authoritatively condemned by means of anathema. It was suppressed but rumbled on below the surface. Today, however, unwanted information that may be generated in an ordinary discussion is automatically removed from the dialogical web and fed back to the sender, as happens with market surveys. The information is reabsorbed and, in this way, reinforces the tendency of the sender to become more and more indistinct and inauthentic. In contrast to the Catholic Middle Ages, discourse today automatically approaches entropy, and only in this modified sense can it be said that we are becoming more catholic (*catholic* = *kata holon* = "for all"). Unless, of course—and this is the point I am about to discuss—the dormant dialogical possibilities of telematic technology were to be used against, rather than in support of, the discursive social structure.

At present, telematic gadgets—all the videos, videogames, videodisks, and cassettes—in fact support the senders that program them. The feeling of emptiness we get from them is justified. It is not their technical construction that causes them to function in this way, however; rather their users are programmed to use them in this way and no other. On the contrary, they are technically constructed to serve a truly dialogic function. Users of gadgets are programmed to distract themselves. Distraction is the contract between images and people. Therefore people use telematic gadgets to distract themselves. This use contradicts the gadgets' inherent technical construction, and only by being used in this way do they become gadgets. If the potential of these telematic resources were to become clear, they could become powerful tools to oppose the discursive society. The reason this hasn't happened yet is that the general agreement favors dispersal and puts assembly at a disadvantage. The unspectacular revolutionaries mentioned earlier are trying to show people that telematic resources could support a general discussion of the current state of separation. The "unspectacular revolutionaries" are convinced that telematic devices will, as a result of the way they are organized, shatter the present consensus and build a new, dialogic one.

For if people turn to telematic technology to use it for conversation, rather than to be distracted by it, then technical images suddenly change character. Suddenly they become surfaces where information is produced and through which people can enter into dialogue. They suddenly play the meditating role that linear texts once played between correspondents: they become letters, except that images can carry infinitely more information than texts. For surfaces consist of infinitely many lines. The art of letter writing is almost lost. Images that can be telematically manipulated could give rise to an art that is still inconceivable, a pictorial dialogue infinitely richer than linear, historical dialogue could ever have been.

Such a society, in dialogue through images, would be a society of artists. It would dialogically envision, in images, situations that have never been seen and could not be predicted. It would be a society of players who would constantly generate new relationships by playing off moves against countermoves, a society of *Homines ludentes* in which inconceivable possibilities would open to human existence. But that is not all. As a result of this creative play and counterplay, a consensus would arise, allowing society to program the apparatuses by means of images. Apparatuses would then serve this broadly human intention, which is to say, to release people from work and free them for play with other people in a way that constantly generates new information and new adventures. I believe this is the utopia that engages the unspectacular revolutionaries.

After this digression, another look at the possibilities that lie dormant in telematic equipment, at the silly twiddling with telematic gadgets, shows where most cultural critics go wrong. They try to criticize the radiating centers to change or do away with them. But revolutionary engagement has to begin not with the centers but with the silly telematic gadgets. It is these that must be changed and changed in ways that suit their technology. Should this be successful, the centers will collapse of their own accord. No longer historical but rather cybernetic categories must be used for criticism.

At the end of the previous chapter, I said that the technical images would have to be reformed to serve a dialogical function quite quickly because otherwise it would be too late. Telematic devices show that this could happen very soon, perhaps even immediately. The silly twiddling with these devices, however, also shows that it is possible to miss the deadline. For the way telematic gadgets are used now, to produce empty chatter and twaddle on a global scale, a flood of banal technical images, definitively cements in place all the gaps between isolated, distracted, key-pressing human beings. Soon there will be nothing more we can say to one another, so now is the moment to talk it over.

To Play

The central problem to be discussed with regard to a dialogic society is that of generating information. It is this problem that was called "creativity" in former times. How do we get information that is unpredictable and improbable? It looks as though it suddenly appears from nowhere, as if it were a miracle. Hence the concept *creatio ex nihilo;* hence the belief in a creator god; and hence the veneration of creative people, above all so-called artists. The problem of generating information must be lifted out of this mythologizing context to grasp the revolutionary possibilities of a telematic society, a true information society.

A mythologizing approach to the problem of information generation seems forced on us. Looking at the world as it appears around us, one cannot repress the feeling of standing in a supermiracle composed of miracles. How did the wonderful organization of the starry heavens come about, an organization whose complexity becomes more amazing the more closely we examine it? The more deeply we probe into the structures of organisms, beginning with protozoa up to the human brain, the more we are gripped with astonishment over the sheer, incredible complexity of the innumerable factors that are in play. And what is there to say of the human brain, into which we are only just beginning to gain some insight, and that is such a complex organ at so many interconnected levels that it seems presumptuous to even attempt to explain it, to say nothing of imitating it? In the face of such a miraculous world, so miraculously put together from such miracles, one cannot initially help ascribing it to a creator. One must acknowledge a few unacceptable things in the creation, such as suffering and death, but who are we, creations that we are, to question the creator's plan?

All these totally improbable situations, like the Milky Way, protozoa, and human brains, all this information must have had some sort of intention we are unable to see to fit into the general configuration of the world. But couldn't one also ask whether another sort of world might have accidentally been produced? And such an impertinent question turns our admiration for the world into its opposite. As an example, suppose the world were just a little bit different, just a very little bit, for example, instead of aluminum, there were another, comparable elements in earth's upper crust. Then, of course, earthly organisms would look completely different, in fact so different that it would make little sense to call them "life." Obviously there could be no talk of human beings or human brains. And yet in the long run, ceteris paribus (all other things being equal), in such a case, something just as complex as protozoa and human brains would necessarily appear.

After this demythologizing question, the world no longer appears as a miraculous creation but as one of very many but not infinitely many chance configurations. The heavenly creator then no longer seems either a necessary or unnecessary hypothesis but one refuted by the world as a play of chance. For then the improbable situations, the world's information, appears to have been randomly generated rather than intentionally fabricated. The human brain, then, no longer appears as part of a plan for the creation but as the result of an accidental biological development that itself came into being accidentally as the result of chemical processes that occur on the earth in one particular pattern and no other. The demythologizing question shows how information in the world and information in general is generated: by synthesizing previous information.

But it shows even more. If information is synthesized from previous information, there must also be an opposing process, namely, information analysis, replacement, and disinformation. And the world shows clearly that there is such a process, so clearly in fact that it takes a mythologizing view of creation to cover it up. All information ultimately disintegrates. Every human brain eventually dissolves into its constituent elements. The species *Homo sapiens,* life on earth, the earth itself will finally follow the world's general tendency to lose information and be dissolved (second law of thermodynamics). And such information decay is more fundamental than information production because information is produced through improbable accidents and decay occurs through probable accidents.

Having demythologized the production of information, we stand face to face with a newly structured universe. It is no longer a creation that emerged from the void and proceeded in linear fashion, step by step ("in six days") toward a predetermined goal, the universe of linear history, but an intractable game of chance in which all possible accidents, including improbable ones, must eventually occur but in which all these possibilities inevitably converge on a probable, uninformed situation, a "heat death."

We no longer face a straight way forward but a path of circles superimposed on one another, linking into one another, epicycles of information that undermine themselves and one another. Rather than composition, one might better speak of the decomposition of the world. We face absurdity. It is relevant here that the apparent linearity of the second law of thermodynamics (everything tends toward entropy) is in fact only a point, namely, that point from which information arises and to which it returns. The linear, historical perspective cannot be preserved in an absurd universe.

Information is a synthesis of prior information. This holds true not only for the information that constitutes the world but also for man-made information. People are not creators but players with prior information, only they, in contrast to the world, play with a purpose to produce information. The evidence for this difference, this intention, is that human information is synthesized far more quickly than so-called natural information. New architectural styles and scientific theories arise from earlier ones much faster than mammals arise from reptiles, for example. And this is because nature plays without purpose, by sheer chance, and human beings play using dialogue.

Dialogues are controlled games of chance. They allow information that is already stored to be combined in all possible ways to construct new information. The word *dialogue* ordinarily suggests a game of chance in which each of two or more memories (usually human brains) tries to synthesize the information stored in the other. But there can also be inner dialogue, in which one memory plays with the information it stores. When it produces new information, such an inner dialogue characterizes what is called, in common usage, a "creative individual." A telematic society would produce a network of dialogues that might be considered an inner dialogue for the whole society. The whole society would be creative in this sense.

No one should think, however, that merely by imagining this playful society, we have escaped the myth of creativity. The mythical is now hidden within the concept of "purpose": what is now secret is that society plays with the purpose of producing information. It is therefore appropriate to defy this concept of "purpose" (which is to say, decision or freedom), despite the risk losing one's bearings. To minimize this danger, I will stick to the following model of the brain: the telematic society as a global superbrain. The first insights into the function of the brain begin to appear. The striking thing is the increasing difficulty in distinguishing between inherited and acquired information, that is, between Lamarck and Darwin. If you look at the brain as an organ for data processing, then the brain itself becomes the hardware, and the processing of data (that which was once called "mind") becomes the software. One could maintain that the hardware brain is inherited genetically and that the software mind is, for the most part, culturally acquired. But such a comparison with a computer is untenable. The organization of the brain changes under the influence of incoming information, and if the stream of incoming information should be interrupted, the brain is irreparably damaged. This has been demonstrated in cats and rats completely isolated from the environment. One is forced to see the human brain as largely a cultural product. On the other hand, one cannot claim that mind is completely acquired. A newborn child has practically no mental processes at all because there are no data to be processed. But structures for basic data processing are in the brain genetically. In short, the brain really is an inherited organ, but it can only function in a cultural situation, and mind really is a cultural phenomenon that cannot exist without a brain.

The question of purpose, the decision or freedom to produce information (process data), must be posed in the context of this new, still fragmentary awareness of brain function. It is already clear, in any case, that we will have to abandon such mythical entities as the "free spirit" or "eternal soul." Purpose cannot sprout from such chimeras. To say that a newborn child has a soul or possesses a spirit is to caricature the rudimentary mental processes under way in its brain. When an electrode is introduced into the brain of an experimental subject and an impulse is sent into a specific part of the brain, this person will do exactly what the experimenter predicts: count to ten and insist on having freely decided to do so. This makes clear that such a decision is the result of an exceptionally complex process involving the computation of incoming with stored information, leading to a specific behavior and changing the brain's structure. And that is true of any kind of decision. The matter can be described as follows: the so-called "I" forms a nexus point in a web comprising streams of information in dialogue, storing information that has passed through. This is in fact the case for both inherited information and for the overwhelming majority of that which is acquired. At this nexus point, unpredictable, improbable computations occur, new information. This new information is experienced as intentional, freely controlled, because each "I" is a unique nexus point, distinguished from all other nexus points in the web by its position and the information it stores. It is not only neurophysiology that presses such an account of intention on us but many insights gained in many other disciplines as well.

If one regards the "I" as a nexus point in a dialogical web, society necessarily appears as a superbrain made up of individual brains. And the telematic society would distinguish itself from earlier societies only insofar as its cerebral-net character has become conscious, enabling us to start consciously manipulating the net structure. The telematic society would be the first to recognize the production of information as society's actual function and so to systematically foster this production: the first self-conscious and therefore free society.

As long as images operate as they do today, our society is a miserable superbrain, supporting a supermind with very little that is superlative, for the current circuit diagram with bundles radiating out from a center has been constructed in keeping with a model of the brain that is long out of date. We now know that the brain is not centrally controlled but governed through an interaction between areas and functions of the brain that are to some extent interchangeable. The form of contemporary society embodies an unsatisfactory and in part incorrect perception of the society's cerebral, netlike character. Mass culture, proliferating kitsch, the descent into boredom, into entropy, are the results of this faulty organization. As a result, the real function of society (of the mind) is thwarted. Rather than producing improbable, adventurous things, contemporary society is close to exhausting the information that is fed into it. It is a stupid society.

Today we have access to deeper insights into brain function and telematic technologies that would permit us to turn a stupid society into a creative one, specifically on the basis of a circuitry that does justice to the interaction among brain functions. In such a social structure, there would be no more broadcast centers. Rather each point of intersection in the web would both send and receive. In this way, decisions would be reached all over the web and, as in the brain, would be integrated into a comprehensive decision, a consensus. That which is known in the biological sciences as the leap from individuation to socialization, for example, the shift from single-celled to multiple-celled organisms or from individual to herd animal, would here be achieved at the level of the mind: intention, decision, freedom. The single "I" would maintain its singularity (as does the single cell in an organism and the single animal in the herd), but the production of information would take place at another level, namely, at the level of society.

The socialization of freedom just described is repugnant because it refutes Judeo-Christian anthropology and all the anthropologies that have followed from it. According to these anthropologies, each person has a core that must be preserved and developed. The socialization of decision making and freedom would threaten this core with dissolution. We now know, however, that this core is a myth and that the anthropologies are untenable. In fact, we know this from completely different disciplines that converge— neurophysiology, depth psychology, informatics, and above all, phenomenological analysis. Eidetic reduction demonstrates that "I" is an abstract hook on which to hang concrete circumstances and that in the absence of those circumstances, the "I" reveals itself to be nothing. A socialization of freedom emphasizes the concrete relations that bind us to one another and so does not threaten to dissolve identity but on the contrary to reveal it. We only really become an "I" if we are there with and for others. "I" is the one to whom someone says "you."

The crucial thing about such a dialogic reordering of society, about this "dialogic life" (Buber), is its playfulness. Society as a dialogical cerebral web must be regarded as a social game, and the information such a society produces must be regarded as moves in a sort of chess game. Nature only produces information by chance, but society produces it purposefully, which is to say, methodically, assuming the play has a strategy. Only the social game, in contrast to the chess game, is an open one, which is to say that rules can change in the course of the game. I will have more to say about a strategy for the future governing of society, about cybernetics, and about the openness of the information-producing game in the course of this essay. Here I will just stay with a possible means of taking the argument further.

A telematic society would be a dialogic game in systematic search of new information. This disciplined search can be called "freedom" and the direction of the search "purpose." The separate pieces of information, as they appear in the course of the telematic play (single, constantly revised technical images), will become increasingly improbable as a result of this strategy. Therefore it is nonsense to try to predict it. What we're seeing on our monitors now, however exciting it may sometimes be, is only a pale shadow of what we could do. As the brain only produces a fraction of what it is capable of producing, so does the telematic society have unforeseeable possibilities. But the telematic society will develop faster than the brain. For the brain appeared as an accident in the natural game of chance, and the new society will appear as one move in a purposefully directed social game. It will arise from the same aleatory play that gave rise to brains, but in these brains, the aleatory play has become strategic, a game of chance that has turned against chance. In short, in the telematic society, it will become clear that the brain has accidentally been built to be capable of countermanding chance. This has always been true of human beings: by coincidence, we are free beings. But in the new society, this human tendency to defy accident, to reject entropy, will develop freely for the first time. For the first time, people will be in a position to methodically generate information, and not only empirical information, using a technology modeled on perception. Information will then surge like a rising tide against entropy. If we define human beings by their negentropic tendency, then this is when they will become truly human for the first time, that is, players with information; and the telematic society, this "information society" in the true sense of the word, will be the first genuinely free society.

To Create

As I was concerned to show in the last chapter, the production of information is a game of assembling existing information. Such an insight into the creative process may destroy the mythical aura of creation but not its unique excitement. On the contrary, this creative inspiration, this going-out-of-oneself into the information to be produced, into an adventure, is exactly what freedom is. That can be seen clearly in creative people of the past and present, whether they were scientists, technicians, philosophers, artists, or activists. They work freshly, without self-regard, from the information they have stored within themselves, and they then put works into society: they publish. They move from themselves into their work. But this way of producing information through inner dialogue cannot be maintained much longer. Even now, most information is produced not by individuals but by groups in dialogue, and as far as the work goes, the concept is undermined by the reproducibility and insubstantiality, the immateriality of technical images. What happens to creative inspiration in the production of a video clip, for example, in which many people participate and where the work, the tape, cannot only be endlessly reproduced but also continually changed? For a telematic society, this is a crucial question. There, all information will be synthesized through intersubjective conversations, will be infinitely reproducible, and will be designed to be changed by its receivers and forwarded as new information. Can there be creative inspiration in such a situation, without author or work? Can there be that disregard of self, that absorption in work that constitutes freedom?

The issue here is first the reproducibility of all generated information. The Latin *copia* means "surplus." *To copy,* therefore, would be "to make superfluous." The question is, what is actually made superfluous by copying? The first answer is that it makes the human labor of repeating existing information (rewriting, redrawing, recalculating) superfluous because copying is done by apparatuses. But that is just the first, harmless answer. Another, and far more dangerous one appears on closer consideration: copying makes all authority and all authors superfluous and so puts creative inspiration to the test. This can be seen, for example, in the problem of copyright in light of the copy shop.

The words *author* and *authority* come from the verb *augere,* meaning "to cause to grow," usually translated, however, as "to establish." Here one has Roman agriculture in mind, where a seed is put in the ground to grow. We are in a Roman myth, in fact this one: the city of Rome has a founder, an "author," Romulus, who put it into the ground so that it could take root and grow to become a world power. Although Romulus is the author of the city and the world *(urbi et orbi),* the city and the world could not grow if they were not doubly connected to their author. These connections are called "authorities." The retroactive (re-ligious) one is the Great Authority *(Magisterium);* the other, which drives the author forward, is the lesser authority *(Ministerium),* and together they form the social structure.

This Latin myth and the authoritative social structures that devolve from it carries over from the Roman Empire to the Church and from there to almost all modern administrative forms. Channels of authority bound up with authors can be recognized everywhere, in the army, in factories, in parties and states. I would suggest at this point that the reproducibility of technical images, in fact of all information, renders this structure superfluous, definitively removing all authority and all authors. That is the so-called crisis of authority, and that is the reason for the increasing rarity of "great people" (authors).

Reproducibility makes all lesser authorities (those who pass messages) superfluous because it enables messages to be passed automatically in vast quantities. The copy shop requires no minister, no press, no publisher, in short no more administration. And reproducibility renders all great authorities (those who guarantee the accuracy of messages) superfluous, for copies are automatically accurate and become even more so as copying technologies improve. In the copy shop, there is no further need for a master, priest (*pontifices* = bridge builders), in short for any religion. Put another way, copying makes administration and religion automatic.

Ministers and masters, for example, publishers and photographers, still defend themselves against this automation. Publishers maintain that automatic copying is blind (without criteria), and publishers must control copy apparatuses to filter the deluge of information. Photographers maintain that automatic copying is inaccurate and that only when they control the apparatus (authorized print) can the copy be faithful to the intended message. Yet both these attempts to rescue authority for the information society are fighting from lost positions. As to the filtering of messages (criticism, censorship), I will come back to this and try to show that the apparatus can do it automatically. As to accuracy, it is a technical question, and there can be no doubt that copies will become clones in the near future. But there is another matter relating to accuracy. In the coming information society, messages are to be synthesized by their receivers into new messages. I contend that despite these objections to my hypothesis, every authority will disappear because reproducibility has made it redundant.

For the moment, copy apparatuses seem sometimes to be copying "originals" (texts, photographs, films), and an "original" is a message that springs from the mouths of authors (from *ora*, "mouths"). Looking more closely, however, one sees how this "mouth" is arranged (Greek: *mythos,* "sound springing from the mouth"). The information does not come from a mythical author but from outer and inner dialogues, in which artificial memories (apparatuses) will play an ever-increasing part. The myth of the author assumes that for significant messages, there are "originals" produced by "great people" as a result of inner dialogues. The mythical author creates in isolation. Of course, one wouldn't want to deny that even the "great person" works in a context containing the information that nourishes him. But one would claim that through the creative effort of the author, something absolutely new appears, something arises from nothing. The myth of the author (and the original) distorts the fact that the production of information is a dialogue. Now that messages are reproducible, this fact can no longer be disguised. A photograph, for example, is the result of a dialogue between the photographer and the photographic apparatus (and a whole series of less obvious conversation partners), and it is ridiculous to call each one of these partners an "author." Given the copy shop and cybernetic control of dialogue, all authors, founders, donors, Moseses, Founding Fathers, and Marxes (including the Holy Creator) have become redundant.

According to the myth, each society is the work of a superhuman hero, a so-called culture hero suspended in isolation, "in the icy heights." Romulus, as the founder of Rome, is only one of countless examples: each tribe of Amazonian Indians has such a creator, often in the form of an animal. Therefore each mythical society is unique and cannot be copied. It would be monstrous even to suppose that a society founded by a mythical wolf could be transposed onto another founded by a condor. Each mythical society is an original and as such the center of a unique universe. The break of modern thinking with the ecclesiastical concept of society of a social form founded by Christ appears in repeated attempts to construct social structures through dialogue, through consensus, without individual founders. These resulted in societies that can be copied (e.g., Western democracies or socialist people's republics). Wherever they have been copied, mythical culture heroes have been deposed. Certainly the methods of conducting such nation-founding, constitutional dialogues have always been empirical so that some of the spokesmen in the dialogue, for example, the Founding Fathers, Robespierre, or Marx, were mythologized retroactively. This was about secondary authors. Today cybernetic theory and telematic practice is beginning to structure such dialogue in a disciplined and systematic way. The rising information society will not have even secondary authors. It is not original and so can be copied automatically anywhere, at any time. And what is true of nation founding is true for all future information. In the future, no creation of any kind will have an author, a foundational totem animal.

It looks as though a telematicized society, characterized by reproducibility of all information, will have no space for creative inspiration, for freedom. Where every message is produced by arrangement, namely, as an answer to a challenge, there can apparently be no free authors, and where every message is generated dialogically and in part through dialogue with apparatuses, it appears that there can be no authors. And as a result, there can be no inspiration to generate information. But this is a false interpretation of the rising information society. The error can be seen in a consideration of how information is synthesized.

The information available to us has astronomical dimensions and has long since passed the point where it can be stored in a human memory. We can expand our memory capacity and store larger and larger fragments of the available information—the average person today knows more than the universal genius of the Renaissance did, but it is more reasonable to store the available information in artificial memories. Furthermore, human memory is too slow to be able to compute a large quantity of information into new information. Data processing is faster by machine. So the inner dialogue has become inoperative. "Great people" can no longer function. Not only are authors no longer necessary, they are not even possible.

Instead, we can have outer dialogue, intersubjective conversations that are disproportionately more creative than any the "great people" could ever have had, dialogues such as those that occur in the laboratory or work team, in which human memories are linked to artificial ones to synthesize information. Already some of the dialogues are producing such quantities of new and sometimes astonishing information as the "great people" of the past could never have dreamed. And the telematicized society will be one giant dialogue of this type, a dialogue in which everyone could theoretically participate.

I will use a chess game to illustrate the spirit that prevails when information is being produced in this way. Apparently chess is a zero-sum game: two opponents play, one wins, the other loses, and the result is nothing ($+1 - 1 = 0$). The strategy of the game is to lure the opponent into traps to defeat him. The word *strategy* comes from *strategos* (commander) and carries the sense of *stratagema* (cunning). So chess appears to be a cunning game of war, ending in nothing. But the actual experience of the game contradicts this. For as the game proceeds, unpredictable, improbable, exciting situations (i.e., informative situations) occur that make chess interesting. In the context of such situations, such "chess problems," a victory becomes uninteresting, and the point rather becomes making the most of them. Both opponents ally themselves against the problem: polemic becomes dialogue. They remember that *stratagema* comes from *stratos,* that is, "level," and that this again comes from the ancient root *str* that we recognize in *distribute.* Their strategy is now to compute the bits of information distributed in the unexpected situation to new levels. And they are inspired. For chess has become a plus-sum game. Both players have gained new information.

The example of the chess game is intended to characterize the emerging *homo ludens,* this playful, telematic existence. It is meant to show what is meant here by a playful strategy, which is not the setting of cunning traps (art in the sense of artifice) but a methodical computing of scattered particle elements (art in the sense of skill). It is meant to show how outer dialogue can be productive.

And above all, it is meant to show how outer dialogues are inspirational. It is meant to show how players, forgetting themselves, happen to produce information, and how the concept of "creative inspiration" therefore refers to that spirit in which global telematic dialogue occurs.

The inner dialogue that was once so exciting can easily be simulated with chess. One sits alone at the board and alternatively moves the white and black pieces. Interesting, informative situations can result. But as soon as a second player joins in, it immediately becomes clear how limited the initial situation was. With the addition of the second player, the competency has doubled. Under pretelematic conditions, including the present, the singular way of playing was responsible for almost all information (scientific, philosophical, artistic, or political). Telematics, on the other hand, will involve very many players in the game, and the playing competence will expand exponentially. All the information generated until now by great individuals (our entire cultural inheritance) will be regarded as relatively sparse in the future. Compared to synthetically produced information of the future, compared above all with future images, the culture of the past will appear as a mere starting point. It will become clear that a systematic, conscious creativity really begins with telematics.

The telematic method of generating information through outer dialogue, through dialogues in which all human beings and all artificial intelligences could theoretically participate by means of cable or satellite, is basically only a technical application of the theoretical perception that all information arises through the computation of bits of information. Telematics is a technology of information production that rests on theory, as, say, the eighteenth-century machine was a theory-based technology for the production of informed objects. We may therefore anticipate a revolution in the field of information production that is in every respect the equal of the Industrial Revolution in the field of object production.

For example, in the Industrial Revolution, vehicles developed slowly, from the log canoe to the three-master ship and from slave porters to the stage coach. Each separate phase of the development had an inventor who was often anonymous but who may have been a god or half god near the beginning. After the Industrial Revolution, this development not only accelerated but its character also changed fundamentally. From the sailboat, not only a steamship and an airplane, and from the stage coach an automobile and a rocket, but the theory that now entered into the picture lifted the process of production from the competence of an inventor into the competence of the impersonal discourse of science and technology. Therefore the three-master ship bears a far stronger resemblance to the log canoe that preceded it by ten thousand years than it does to the rocket, which follows by only two hundred years. With the introduction of theory into the production process, a new order of object was achieved in a single bound, and the life of a man of the eighteenth century A.D. resembled that of a man living in the eighteenth century B.C. far more closely than it did that of his grandson.

A comparable leap is currently under way in the field of information production. Before the information revolution, there was a slow development of, for example, pictures, from cave painting in Lascaux to film, or in music, from the drum to the electronic synthesizer. Each individual phase of this development is credited to a great artist who was often nameless but who may have been a god in the first phases and, in the most recent ones, was a gifted creator type such as Cézanne or Mozart. After the Information Revolution, this development will not only accelerate but will acquire a fundamentally different character. Not only will there be images and music we never dreamed of, drawing on a wealth of information never dreamed of, but the information theory that is now brought to bear will lift the production process out of the competence of the individual creator into the competence of interpersonal dialogue. Therefore contemporary films resemble the cave paintings at Lascaux more closely than they do images of fractal equations on computer screens. And our lives resemble those of our eighteenth-century ancestors more closely than they do those of our grandchildren. For genuinely disciplined, theorized creativity will only be possible after the myth of the author of information is abandoned.

By introducing a theory of the production process, the empirical factor (intuition, inspiration, heuristic experiment) will not be neutralized or superseded; on the contrary, it will unfold to its full extent for the first time. The dynamics of technical innovation derive from the complex exchange between theory and observation, on one hand, and theory and experimentation, on the other. Intuition, inspiration, and heuristic experiment are all at play in developing a Concorde, to a degree the inventor of the stagecoach could never have grasped. Inspiration and intuition can only be tested in the raster of theory, and in this sense, the Concorde is a far greater work of art than the stagecoach could be. Something similar can be expected from images that will be synthesized in the future. Creative inspiration only really becomes visionary power when it runs up against the raster of theory, as embodied in apparatuses. Future images will be art at a high level because they will owe their production to this dialectic between the theory embedded in the apparatuses and the intuitive hallucinatory power of the envisioners.

The telematic society will not therefore abolish creation but will, on the contrary, invest it with its real meaning. Creation there will not be limited to a few "great people" who produce informative works empirically by means of a lonely inner dialogue. The time for such creative individuals, such heroes, is definitively past: they have become superfluous and impossible at the same time. One should add that the time of history (in the sense of linear consequence of *res gestae*[1]) is definitively past. Instead everyone will participate in the creative process and test their intuitions and inspirations against the theories embodied in apparatuses, of whose riches we as yet have no inkling. This information will no longer comprise works, objects, but messages without substance, challenges to everyone to continually produce new information from them. And yet this information will be more eternal than historical works, for not only can it be reproduced eternally but it can also be stored in eternal memories. Only when we stop thinking of the work, of information engraved in an object (i.e., when we get past the materiality of information, subject to the second law of thermodynamics), can we even begin to create anything immortal.

The person of the future, playing at the keyboard, will be ecstatic about the creation of durable information that is nevertheless constantly available for a new synthesis. We can see this ecstasy in its embryonic form in children who sit at terminals. The person of the future will be absorbed in the creative process to the point of self-forgetfulness. He will rise up to play with others by means of the apparatuses. It is therefore wrong to see this forgetting of self in play as a loss of self. On the contrary, the future being will find himself, substantiate himself, through play. The "I" that eidetic reduction (and neuropsychological, psychological, and informatic analysis) has shown to be an abstract concept, to be nothing, will be realized for the first time through creative play. The playing person will find himself in others through creative play. In this conversation, in this creative play of mutual recognition of the other, all are on equal, familiar terms. That is what is meant here by *play,* by *create,* and by *telematic.*

These utopian thoughts are themselves caught up in the delirium of play. And so they hope to be received, changed, and sent on by the receiver in the same playful spirit.

To Prepare

The question of freedom, of the capacity to deliberately decide to be informed, has run like a red thread, unanswered, through these reflections. For looking at the difference between natural and cultural information production from the outside, as a matter of degree (culture produces the unexpected more often than nature does), we arrive at a diluted freedom: what a human being achieves through strategic play may be achieved by nature as well, but it takes longer. And in seeing this difference from the inside, so to speak, as that between an implacably automatic nature and a creatively inspired human being, we come to regard freedom as subjective: we do experience our information as intentionally produced. But from a higher position, information such as a computer cannot be distinguished from information such as an amoeba on the basis of freedom because both arise as a synthesis of previous information. Perhaps the question of freedom can be posed more satisfactorily by trying to capture the difference between random and strategic computation at the moment both are generating new information, in that instant when new information appears, that is, not by comparing the computer with the amoeba but the rise of the computer with the rise of the amoeba.

At first glance, it looks as though improbable situations occur under completely random natural conditions as leaps, one after the other, and so become increasingly improbable, as if nature were a staircase in which each step is less improbable than the last, and more probable than the next. The information available at each step is randomly computed to new information, which rises out of that step to form the next one. And nature's progress would appear discontinuous. This gives the impression of a "natural history." Say, increasingly complex atoms come from particles (a more complex atom arises from a simpler one), from atoms come more complex molecules (a more complex molecule arises from a simpler one), from molecules come more complex organisms (a more complex one arises from a simpler one), and a human being, as the highest level reached so far, is curiously able to write this natural history. By focusing attention on the moment in which the one step arises from the other, however, natural history, understood as discontinuous progress, disappears. To ask, for example, what really happens to an oxygen atom to turn it into a helium atom? or what actually happens to a reptile to turn it into a primate? The answers do not accommodate discontinuous progress. At each step, the answer will be different from all others. Still, it is possible to recognize a common ground. For at each step, coincidences are constantly occurring that dismantle this step. The oxygen atom is always about to disintegrate into particles and the reptile to degenerate through random mutations in its genetic information. Once it is achieved, each level of information is in constant decay. There are also some very rare accidents that lead to the next informational level, but this new level begins to disintegrate the moment it has appeared. In nature, we are concerned with a staircase in constant decay as a whole and at each step.

That is what is meant by the claim that nature is random: it falls apart, yields to entropy. And this disintegration is aleatory to such a degree that even in the ruins, new information is always emerging. If the concept of "emergence" is popular today, it is against such a broad backdrop of ruins.

If you compare natural history with cultural history, that is, the random with the strategic production of information, intentional creation (freedom) appears in a new light. The difference then appears neither as a question of speed (as if history had been accelerating since the advent of mankind) nor as a question of one's perspective (as if cultural history were nothing but natural history from a human point of view) but as a reversal of direction (natural history runs toward decay, cultural history starts from decay); that is, human engagement no longer looks like a better method of producing information, nor does it look like a natural disposition. Rather it looks like an engagement against nature and above all against the inevitable natural decay of information, against death, against being forgotten. We produce information to avoid being forgotten, and to be free is to confront death.

In comparing cultural history with natural history, it does appear that in both cases, a discontinuous progress is occurring amid general ruin. Even in cultural history, each new level of information begins to decay as soon as it appears. The Baroque had scarcely emerged from previous information, for example, before signs of decay became noticeable in it. And in cultural history, too, everything is prey to oblivion. Not only will everyone die, most having been forgotten, but cities, too, will fall, and there have undoubtedly been whole cultures that have been forgotten forever. Nevertheless, the tendency of cultural history is opposed to that of natural history. In nature, new information appears as an error, so to speak, as an unpredictable accident (in biology, mutations are discussed as errors in the transfer of information). And in culture, being forgotten is the accident, an accident that has, by the way, proven unavoidable so far. So the central problem in the intentional production of information is that of not being forgotten, of memory.

From this standpoint, telematics can be regarded as a technology that permits all fabricated information to be stored in permanent memory. In telematic dialogues, human and artificial memories exchange information to synthesize new information and to store it artificially. In this way, not only the new information but also the human memories that produced it are protected from oblivion. The real intention of telematics is to become immortal. For telematics fosters an awareness that freedom lies not only in producing information but also in preserving this information from natural entropy—that we create not to die.

This is not new. There have always been attempts to put information in permanent storage *(aere perennis)* or at least in media that degenerate very slowly such as bronze or marble. But it was always a lost cause, for all storage media, because they are material, which is to say natural, are subject to the second law of thermodynamics and must decay along with the information they carry. Only since the advent of electromagnetic images, immaterial, pure information, can we hope to escape the curse of being forgotten. Only now can we fabricate memories over which nature has no power. Telematic society is the first answer to the previously inevitable decay of all culture and everything associated with it into the void of oblivion, into death. And it is a technical answer.

All information must decay if it is stored in a material medium. Once this is accepted, all linear models of history must be abandoned. History is then no longer a linear process of human beings transforming nature into culture. The situation is rather this: human beings progressively tear things from nature to impress information into them, that is, to turn them into cultural objects. Cultural objects produced in this way are used up, that is, the information embedded in them is washed out. Such used cultural objects are thrown away, and they form waste. There the information remaining in them decays through entropy, and the object returns to the nature from which it was initially torn. For example, an animal skin is taken from nature, and information is impressed on it: the cultural object "shoe" is produced. The shoe is worn, loses its information, and is thrown into the rubbish. There it decays according to the second law of thermodynamics and returns to an amorphous mass in that very nature from which it was initially drawn. We are looking at a cycle of nature–culture–waste–nature, with no thought of linear progress. All progressive historicism must be abandoned.

Engaged against the degenerative cycle nature–culture–waste–nature, against the decay of information, human beings devise more and more durable supports, for example, plastic bottles instead of glass ones. But perversely, this halts the degenerative cycle not at the point of remembering but at the point of waste, of forgetting. The plastic bottle is discarded just as quickly as the glass one but lasts longer before returning to nature. Waste accumulated in this way contaminates the environment, seeps back into culture, and threatens to flood it with recycled, half-forgotten things, with kitsch. In answer to this threat, sciences of the discarded, such as ecology, archaeology, depth psychology, and etymology, have arisen alongside the sciences and humanities. They seek to recall the half forgotten, to master the discarded material, a typical posthistorical problematic.

Telematics will put an end to this problematic situation that currently threatens us, for it will permit information to be generated and stored without a material support. Immaterial supports such as electromagnetic fields do not decay into waste, and the information embedded in them can be kept in cultural memory indefinitely. The cycle nature–culture–waste–nature will be halted at culture, not waste. As a result of the new opportunity to store information without material support, interest in material supports as information carriers will diminish radically. If I have access to a video library, why should I want to store ten pairs of shoes in the closet? I will prefer to have as few objects as possible to have space to store my videocassettes, and these few objects will have to be as impermanent and disposable as possible. No plastic bottles, that is, but paper bottles. Waste will be reduced to a minimum, specifically to the minimum of essential objects of use, and it will return to nature quickly. Telematics will solve the problem of waste in this way, for it will allow us to disregard material supports for information.

It will, on the other hand, present another, equally threatening problem. For if the circular pattern nature–culture–waste–nature begins to stall at culture rather than at waste, we will require a vast store for culture to provide storage for the flood of incoming information. Otherwise we will suffocate from a surfeit of information rather than of waste. It is already possible to see, in rough outline, what such a cultural reconstruction would look like. First, increasingly efficient artificial memories will be integrated into the culture. Second, the concept of "forgetting" will have to acquire a new and fully adjustable meaning. Forgetting must achieve equal status with learning and be recognized as equally critical to information strategy. Third, it will become possible to delete redundant information (that which is already stored elsewhere) from specific memories. Redundant and informative situations will have to be systematically distinguished. For the time being, none of these methods is adequate to the excess of accessible information. In the distant future, this excess will become a primary concern because in contrast to sources of raw materials and energy, sources of information spring eternal.

For telematic culture to achieve such a reordering of the cultural cycle, all the information previously stored on paperlike supports (especially texts and pictures) will have to be made electromagnetic. This translation from chemistry to electronics is already in progress. Photographs, films, and books are migrating to terminals, however unaware those affected may be. This technical revolution, which will cause chemical supports such as printer's ink or silver compounds to disappear, will certainly affect writing and image making. Those who write and make images will have to become envisioners. To put it another way: all contemporary technical images, but also all contemporary texts, should be regarded as harbingers of synthetic computer images. Only when the translation into the electromagnetic field is finished will we actually be able to store information in permanent memory to reproduce and transform it again there. Only then will information be not only safe but also constantly productive of new information. And so strategic, dialogical play with pure information will at last be set in opposition to nature's blind play of chance, making us immortal.

That is the intention of telematics. The question is, what strategy will bring it about? Or in other words, what exactly is the difference between blind natural chance and the strategy of dialogue, that is, between entropy and negentropy, between inevitable coincidence and freedom? The answer lies in the fact that chance will inevitably combine all information, whereas in dialogue, redundant information will be erased. Freedom is essentially the difference between that which is redundant and that which is actually information, and the free person is the one who is competent to decide.

Before I pursue the question of competence, I will give two examples, the discovery of how to make fire and the Newtonian worldview, that is, two exceptionally improbable, unforeseeable, and so highly informative situations. What made Stone Age people competent to start fires and Newton to develop his understanding of the world? Both appear to have played with chance, exactly as nature does. They latched on to accidents (such as a tree struck by lightening or an apple that fell on Newton's head as he slept; in the second example, *si non é vero, é ben trovato*[1]). They did not select an accident by chance, however, but because they recognized in it a model of an entirely improbable situation. A chance occurrence became something that occurred to them. The Stone Age man was competent to recognize in the event "burning tree" a model for an extremely improbable condition of a "cooking and therefore meat-eating primate," and in this way, he transformed human beings into hunters of large game. Newton was competent to recognize in the falling apple a model for the fusion of Galileo's mechanics with Kepler's astronomy, and in this way, he founded modern physics. Both were competent to turn a redundant accident into unforeseeable information. Both were free. But how did they acquire this competence? How did they become free?

In a time before telematics, mythical answers held sway. There were exceptional individuals, born geniuses. There were "authors." Even then, one had to admit that this inherited information, this gift, was insufficient to produce "fire" or "Newtonian physics." Newton, for example, had to have known mechanics and astronomy to appreciate the falling apple incident. But it was still assumed that not all those who learned mechanics and astronomy would become Newton. Telematics teaches us something better: anyone can become Newton. To achieve such competence, it is necessary only to have participated in dialogical play. Dialogical play is a preparation for competencies, and participating players are made ready to transform redundancies into information. If only a few people were geniuses in the pretelematic era, it was because most people were unable to participate in dialogue; rather they had to impress the information that had been generated in dialogue onto material supports: they had to "work." By freeing people from the need to work, telematics and robotics will free humanity to be original, to be competent to transform the redundant into the informative. Robotics provides the requisite leisure *(schole)* to turn telematics into a school for competencies, a school for freedom.

The concept of "competence" is, in fact, a mathematical concept, and it can be quantified, but in this context, it takes on an existential coloration. Competence is the sum of all possible combinations (computations) of elements according to rules. For example, the competence of a chess game is the sum of all possible arrangements of the chess pieces according to the rules of play, and this competence is larger than that of checkers. Or the competence of a camera is the sum of all possible photographs that follow the rules programmed into the apparatus, and this competence becomes greater with each new apparatus. Or the competence of an English speaker is the sum of all possible combinations of English words in his vocabulary that follow the rules of the language, and it increases whenever he learns new words and rules. The sum of elements in the repertoire and the sum of rules in the structure can be called "competence," and one can say that competence is the function of a given repertoire in a given structure. Competence increases when repertoire and/or structure increases. For human beings, the structure of data processing is, put simply, the brain, and it is extremely large, so large that the greatest part of it lies fallow. Human competence increases when the repertoire (data) increases. And that is the goal that telematics has set.

The thing that is immediately interesting about the play of telematic dialogue is not that previously unimaginable quantities of new information will appear but that everyone who participates will be prepared for this production, that they will all be competent to turn redundancies into information, that a whole society of geniuses, fire-finders, Newtons will result from such dialogue. In theory, everyone will be telematically prepared and competent to produce more and more improbable, adventurous information. That is the strategy of freedom: information exchange with the purpose of raising the competence to transform redundant coincidence into the unforeseeable, into an adventure.

This strategy has, unfortunately, an unpleasant side, for it applies to artificial intelligences as well as human beings. Telematics can steadily increase the competence not only of all human beings but also of all artificial intelligences, and these artificial intelligences will also become more like geniuses. So the question of how human intelligence and artificial intelligence are related will become the center of the dialogue very soon. We will face the unpleasant choice between humanizing artificial intelligences and making human ones more like apparatuses. But this may be only a pretelematic view of the question. In telematic dialogue, human and artificial intelligences will be connected in such as a way as to make it meaningless to try to distinguish between the human and artificial factors involved in producing information. Artificial and human intelligences will merge into a unity in a way that can be seen now in embryonic form between photographer and camera. The freer people become, the more competent the computers to which they are connected. The more refined the artificial intelligence, the greater the visionary power of the people who produce images in collaboration with it. Of course, this human–apparatus connection must be truly dialogical and not one in which the human being is programmed by the apparatus, as things stand now. In the chapter "To Celebrate," I will have more to say about such a dialogical programming (so-called self-programming). From the perspective of a truly operative telematic society (not from the standpoint of the present apparatus–human being circuit), increasingly competent apparatuses lead to increasingly competent people.

Telematic society is a school for freedom, freedom as a human engagement in producing information against entropy, decay, death. And yet to be free, does one have to want to be free? Before anyone made a photograph, and before anyone was competent to photograph, didn't someone have to have wanted to photograph? Does telematic society not rest on this commitment to freedom, without which it becomes nonsense? I will devote another chapter to a reflection on freedom in the hope that it will not lead us into the void of infinite regress.

To Decide

The foregoing discussion of the problem of freedom in the coming telematic society offers something like the following picture of this society: it is like a dialogical net through whose threads information runs from knot to knot, broadly resembling a nervous system and specifically resembling a brain. The knots of this net are human and artificial intelligences, where the information accumulates to be stored, computed into new information, and finally sent on toward other knots. The sum of the information available in the net increases steadily. Therefore the net must be regarded as an unnatural system. For in nature—viewed as a system—the sum of available information steadily decreases. In the previous chapter, this unnatural character of the telematic net was seen as an expression of human freedom. Freedom was understood there as a decision to oppose natural entropy. In other words, telematic society was seen as a technology derived from the human will to free itself from the second law of thermodynamics, from decay, from oblivion, from death. Furthermore, it was seen as the last of all such technologies and as the first with a chance of achieving its goal.

To the extent they represent human rather than artificial memories, the knots in the telematic net are known in ordinary language as the "I." In more or less isolated, pretelematic memory, in the individual brain, the stored information is subject to random loss, exactly as it is in atoms, in molecules, and in organisms. The human brain is a natural organ, just as an amoeba is a natural phenomenon, and like an amoeba, it must conform to a natural tendency toward entropy. So that which is called the "I" in ordinary language inevitably forgets and is forgotten if it is not part of a dialogical net. It is true that new information can occur in memory, in the "I," just as it does in molecules or in an amoeba, but these negatively entropic accidents are in turn forgotten. It is true that there is a difference between molecules and amoebae, on one hand, and human memory, on the other. Human memory happens to be constructed in such a way as to strive against forgetting and being forgotten. The "I," the human being, happens to be a free being. And this, its freedom, is the source of all technologies and, finally, of telematics.

Telematic society is the first to be conscious of the intention of all technologies. In contrast to all previous forms of dialogue, it methodically seeks to increase the sum of available information. In all dialogue, we are concerned with technologies aimed at increasing the sum of information in the interpersonal web rather than allowing it to decrease as it would naturally. But telematics is the first to make a method out of this intention to generate the improbable. The crucial question pertaining to all dialogue—why does dialogue produce mainly informative situations rather than mainly situations that lose information, as is the case in nature?—presents itself to telematics with particular urgency. It should be formulated as follows: how does telematic technology systematically lose all redundant information and retain only the informative, that is, how does it filter the stream of information passing along its pathways? This question presumes another: how does telematic technology distinguish between redundancy and information, how does it decide in favor of information, and what criteria does it use as a filter? These criteria, this filter, this decision are the roots of freedom. For the design and construction of this unnatural filter, these criteria, are the gestures of a decision not to forget, not to be forgotten, and not to die.

The question leads us to the set of variations of chance events, namely, accidents, coincidences, mishaps, and occurrences. All dialogues set up filters that rule out unfortunate accidents and mishaps, allowing only lucky coincidences, windfalls into the net. Obviously all these variations of accident are value laden: in saying *criterion,* we mean *values.* But for now my plan is to lift the question of the filter, of the decision, out of the context of values, to proceed as though the filters did not entail ethical and aesthetic decisions.

If two containers have a channel between them, and hot water goes into one container, cold water into the other, after a certain time, there will be lukewarm water in both. That is natural and illustrates the second law of thermodynamics. If the channel is fitted with a filter that allows only the cold molecules from the hot water and the hot molecules from the cold water to pass through, after a time, there will be even hotter water on one side and even colder water on the other. Such a filter can be called "Maxwell's devil." And one can say of this filter that it establishes a dialogue between the two containers that leads to an improbable situation, to information. Seen in this way, this unnatural connection illustrates human dialogue as such, and telematic dialogue in particular.

Maxwell's devil is a mechanism, and an automatic mechanism at that. Not only does it filter automatically, it also decides automatically which molecules will be allowed to pass. And it arrives at this decision on the basis of a difference between hot and cold molecules, recognized in turn automatically with the help of a thermometer. In Maxwell's devil, we therefore have before us an automatic censor and critic. Of course, this automatic critic has to have been programmed by Maxwell beforehand. He has to have been instructed that only hot molecules are to be admitted from the right and only cold ones from the left. This begs the question whether Maxwell was himself programmed to program his devil.

At first, one gets the impression that such automatic critics and censors could only be used for so-called value-free information, that is, only for situations in which apparatuses such as a thermometer can make decisions. When ethical, political, or aesthetic information is at issue, it seems, such apparatuses may not be used. How can such an apparatus be capable of deciding which is the best model of behavior and which film is more beautiful to allow only good and beautiful information into the dialogical net? On first impression, it seems impossible that values could be calibrated as on a thermometer.

But that is an error. Informatics, on one hand, and propositional calculus, on the other, teach us otherwise. Informatics shows that the information content of a given situation is, in principle, precisely measurable, whatever type of information it may be. It is enough to transpose the equation of the second law of thermodynamics into its mirror opposite. Then the rarity of each element of the situation to be measured (the rarity of each bit of information) can be exactly determined. And these measurements can be undertaken at however many levels of a situation one wishes. For example, a German text is to be measured for its information content. In German, X is a rare letter, and the more frequently it occurs in the text to be measured, the more informative this text would become at the level of letters, and the more E occurs, the more redundant at this level. The text could also be measured at the level of words, sentences, rhythms, or styles, however, without introducing any criterion other than rarity. And of course, the same may be done with all types of information, for example, for images. One need only set up such an automatic measuring device as Maxwell's devil, and the decision as to what passes through and what does not occurs automatically. It becomes solely a question of technology. Information does in fact consist of so many levels that it is not humanly possible to single out each one and measure it, but artificial intelligences can calculate and compute faster. If technology moves in this direction (and it is doing so now), then automatic critics will not only replace but will also have deeper insights than human ones in the foreseeable future.

Propositional calculus teaches that values can be calculated. Values are imperatives, should propositions. For example, respecting the life of one's neighbor implies, among other things, the imperative "thou shalt not kill!" All propositions of any sort, including imperatives, can be translated into functional propositions. Functional propositions are a type of indicative and can be formulated as if-then propositions, for example, "if it is raining, I'll take an umbrella." In translating a should proposition into an if-then proposition, it becomes clear that something is missing: from "thou shalt not kill!" we get "if you kill, then . . ." Of course, it is not difficult to fill in the missing part, say, "if you kill, you will go to hell, or to prison, or be court-marshaled or whatever." But should propositions are defective propositions and therefore meaningless. They contain about the same level of information as a dog barking. As soon as the missing functional piece is added, they become calculable. In other words, proposition calculus shows that values are nonsense and that at the point of acquiring a meaning, they stop being qualities and become quantifiable. For example, "if you kill ten times, you will go to prison for life or get a medal for bravery or whatever." Such automatic measuring devices can be fitted into Maxwellian devils, and the decision regarding which values (whether ethical or aesthetic) to permit and which to reject is then made automatically.

Seen from this point of view, telematics appears to be a technology that replaces human beings not only in the creative process but also in the decision-making process. In an earlier chapter, I tried to show that even now, most decisions are made automatically, long before informatic technology and the methods of propositional calculus have reached maturity, and long before telematics has actually become functional. From this standpoint, then, telematics does not look so much like a revolution in the production of information or a revolution in preparation for this production but rather like a revolution in decision making, as a displacement of critical consciousness from human being to automata. The end of freedom.

If this were the correct standpoint, it would be literally unbearable. As critics, as beings who decide, we would be deposed. Fortunately, there is a flaw in the position described earlier, however accurately it diagnoses current tendencies. This flaw lies at that point where it seems there must be a Maxwell to program the devil. By this I am not referring to the banal (and incorrect) conception of a human programmer necessarily standing behind any program; rather I mean that there is not only a programmed decision but also a decision about whether to decide in a programmed way. Here we encounter the danger pointed out earlier, that the question of freedom entails a risk of falling into the void of infinite regress. I will try to avoid this.

The decision to produce automatic critics is, in the first instance, a decision to clearly separate the production from the evaluation of information. For in a pretelematic context, these are combined. There the producer decides which of his insights to put into the dialogical net (publish) and which to withhold. And this decision is made not only after the information is produced but repeatedly as it is happening, as, say, a painter steps back from a painting in progress to evaluate it. This concerns a kind of schizophrenia, a split consciousness, and it can be resolved in a telematic context. For there, the gesture of producing information can be given over to apparatuses, leaving human beings free to focus on evaluation. The photographer, for example, can leave the process of making the image to the blind camera and concern himself with the construction of a filter that either accepts or rejects images made in this way. Müller-Pohle's book *Transformance*[1] is an example. In other words, the automation of production permits everyone to become a critic. And in considering button pressing in this light, one recognizes pure criticism, a decision from which an automatic function follows.

Second, the question arises where such critical evaluation, no longer concerned with production, should be located in the dialogical net. Should it be in front of the information-inducing keyboard, at the receiver's terminal, somewhere in the channel between terminals, or at all these points? This is the question that was known as internal and external criticism in the pretelematic context, as self-censure and censure of others, and so it necessarily posed a question of freedom. In a telematic context, it becomes a technical question. What made the question so urgent in the pretelematic context was that external criticism, the censure of others (i.e., the filters in the channels that regulated information according to criteria), could never be made to coincide with those of self-criticism or self-censure. In a telematic context, however, the channels are reversible. When all human beings are critics, they are critics both of themselves and of all others. In fact, it is only in this dialogic critique that information arises in the first place. In short, in a telematic context, critics will be located wherever this is technically possible.

And this brings us to the third question: wouldn't it be possible to automate this critique so that people wouldn't have to check all the information running in the net for its informational content? Such automata would guarantee the negatively entropic character of all dialogue. They would automatically not only eliminate everything redundant, all gossip, all kitsch, but also erase it from memory, as if such accidents and excesses had never happened; that is, these automatic critics, having been calibrated to quantitative criteria for information and logic, would turn the previous function of criticism around in such a way that instead of allowing what is informative to get through, what is allowed through would be informative (it can easily be confirmed that this reversed function of criticism is already being practiced). And people would then be free to make only the crucial decisions, those metajudgments relating to the programming of the automatic critics. These are, I think, the three steps to the installation of Maxwell's devil, discussed earlier, steps toward greater freedom.

We now recognize that these steps lead into the void. For where all criteria are quantified and objective, there is nothing left requiring metadecisions to be made about it. Neither counterargument nor metadecision can reprogram a computer that has decided to steer a moon rocket on one rather than another course. And yet this does not mean that automatic critics will replace us as decision-making beings. For because all automatic critics will be bound up with one another as well as with all other human beings, all decisions will be made as a function of all other decisions. I plan to look more closely at this cybernetic mode of decision making in the next chapter. Here I will only hypothesize that in such a cybernetic situation, human beings necessarily inherit the right of veto. For only they, and not artificial intelligences, are capable of saying no to all of it, and not because human beings started it all, but because they transcend it all in the following sense: they are capable of abstracting (at this point in the argument, I refrain from venturing further into the void of infinite regress).

In a telematic society, we will in fact be replaced, step by step, by automata as producers and critics of information, but we will maintain the right to say no. Human beings' negatively entropic opposition to nature will proceed automatically, but not necessarily with their automatic participation. All human decisions will become unnecessary in the future and will have a disturbing or dysfunctional effect when they do occur, but they will always have the potential, theoretically at every moment, to stop everything. And this command to stop, this veto right, this right to say no is the negative decision we call "freedom."

The negativity of basic freedom should not be demonized. It should not be identified with the Mephistophelian formula "I am the spirit that always says no."[2] We are free because are able to say no to everything and commit suicide. It is not suicide itself that is freedom, however, but its availability as an option at any moment—not constant rejection, but the constant possibility of rejecting. That is why telematics is a technology of freedom: because it frees us, step by step, of all conditions, even of having to make decisions, and so steadily broadens our view of the fundamental freedom to reject telematics itself. With this awareness, we can confidently embark on the telematic adventure. Even if we are not magistrates and censors, we will remain arbiters.

To Govern

In the universe of technical, telematic images, there is no place for authors or authorities. Both have become superfluous through the automation of production, reproduction, distribution, and judgment. In this universe, images will govern the experience, behavior, desire, and perceptions of individuals and society, which raises the question, what does *govern* mean when no decisions need to be made and where administration is automatic? In a telematic society, does it still make sense to speak of government, of power and the powerful? I will attempt to answer by way of etymology, that is, by way of the roots of those languages in which a millennium of our experience is stored.

One immediately confronts the curious pairing of words *government–Regierung*. The word *government* is from the Greek verb *kybernein,* meaning "to steer," and can be recognized in *cybernetics*. The German word *Regierung* is from the Latin-Etruscan noun *rex,* meaning "king," and its root is the ancient *rg,* meaning "right." At this first glance, then, *government* is concerned with steering, taxation, and tax collection and *Regierung* with jurisprudence and institutions. The opposite of *government* would be a rudderless ship, adrift in the wind and waves (guided by chance), and the opposite of *Regierung* would be lawlessness and injustice (the chaos of chance). Because both concepts are concerned in some way with opposing chance, they are regarded in dictionaries as translatable from one to the other. But in fact, *government* means "steering" and *Regierung* means "judgment," so expressions such as "just government" or "left *Regierung*" are like squared circles.

Chance can be considered from two perspectives.

The German word *Macht* (power) comes from the verb *mögen* (to want, to wish), whose substantive form is *Möglichkeit* (possibility). The English *power* comes from the Latin verb *posse,* meaning "to be able." The French *pouvoir* and Portuguese *poder* also come from *posse,* but they are verb substantives and would really have to be translated into German as *Können* (skill). German does, however, have a substantive of *Können,* namely, *Kunst* (art), so that *pouvoir* should be translated as "art" rather than as "power." All these concepts bring us to a level of awareness where possibilities swing between probable and improbable and where art turns probabilities into improbabilities. And so *Macht* comes to mean the art that exploits improbable accidents to inform.

The German word *herrschen* (to govern) comes from *Herr* (master, lord), meaning *höher* (higher). This sense of superiority is better concealed in the English *domination.* It comes from the Latin *domus* (house) and means the subordination, taming, or domestication of nature through the *dominus,* or master of the house. The household is to be regarded as a framework with compartments (*leges,* "laws") into which the master orders the produce. *To govern,* then, means to set up an order of priorities with the purpose of giving form to a masterless chaos, this no-man's-land of a world. *To govern* means "to institute form, to inform."

The venture into etymology has shown, as one might have guessed, that all the concepts under consideration—government, *Regierung, Macht,* power, *herrschen,* and domestication—share an underlying meaning; that is, they all refer to an engagement against the chaos of randomness (against anarchy) and for form. They all show, at their core, that politics is an art, if "art" is taken to be a method of imposing form on what is formless. All concepts are, in essence, informatic concepts, and it appears that they will fully achieve their meaning only in a telematic society. For are technical images not precisely such an imposition of form on that which is formless?

The question of what political structure will be like in a telematic society, whether there will be a government, power, now takes on a different tone. If politics is understood to be the art of informing, then the question becomes how rather than what: in a telematic society, how does governing, the exercise of power, the administration of justice occur? To go straight to the obvious answer, cybernetically. I am defining *cybernetic* here—without claiming general applicability—as automatic guidance and control of complex systems to take advantage of improbable accidents and to generate information.

There are signs everywhere that we are fast approaching a cybernetically governed society, that society, in fact, has already begun to change into a cybernetically governed one. There can be no doubt that the structure of the emerging society increasingly resembles that of a brain. The notion of technical images as a kind of secretion of a global nervous system, the dreaming of a superbrain, comes to mind. And these secretions, these dreams, can be grasped as the cybernetic governance of brain function. In short, the notion that arises here is that of a dreaming global brain controlled cybernetically through technical images. That would be a metaphor for the telematic society, and it may not even be so metaphorical as it first appears.

I now intend to enter into the domain of images from the standpoint of future telematicized people, to test this domain existentially. I therefore place myself in the universe of technical images rather than at the entrance to this universe, as I have up to this point. I sit at my terminal, receive information in the form of electronic images, and I manipulate them using the keys, changing them and sending them on. I cannot, that is, see my universe by looking right or left, up or down. The picture glowing on the monitor controls me. But I have no need to look around, for anything I wish to see can be made visible to me by my terminal.

If I press on certain buttons, for example, the past is made present for me: I can be present at the founding of Rome, the discovery of

America, or the ovens of Auschwitz. Of course, I know that I am looking at a video disk and not the actual event, but I also know that I am seeing it in a far more concrete form than was with case with earlier history books. For if I do not accept a particular event, I need only press on several other buttons to change it: instead of Columbus, I could have Plato discovering America. For there is no more history, there is only a past accessible in memory and so available in the present.

If I press on still other keys, all the models appear on the screen that explain this present past or past present—all the myths and scientific models that have ever been conceived, from the Aristotelian to modern physics, from Democritus to Marx, from Socrates to Freud. Using the appropriate keys, I will be able to compute all these models to see to what extent they complement or contradict one another. For example, I can build a Catholic–Freudian–Marxist model and, of course, add my own elements to it. My imaginative powers allow me to play with all theories.

And with the appropriate keys, I can also project everything present, whether event or theory, into the future and so make it, too, present. The artificial intelligence behind my terminal is programmed to calculate probability. It can displace Auschwitz into the thirtieth century and project forward all the models implicit in Freud. All these possibilities are available to me in the present on my screen. And I myself can, just by pressing the appropriate buttons, affect this future by adding my own bits of information. For when everything has become present, there is no more future. What once was the future is now a set of possibilities for play in the present.

All information is available to me in an instant. I can, with the appropriate press of a key, blend Rheims Cathedral with Lincoln Center, synthesizing new information in the process. Or I can translate the comparisons used by Jesus into pictures and coordinate them with Bach cantatas. In short, the whole universe awaits me at my terminal as a gigantic playground.

But as fascinating as such play may be, it is only peripheral to the universe I inhabit. By pressing the right button, for example, I can understand what has never been understood before and both see and understand what has never been seen before. The artificial intelligence behind my terminal is programmed to make concepts clear, for example, fractal equations or the concept of dialectical materialism. And it can analyze a performance into concepts as well, for example, a tennis match into equations of motion or a myth of the Bororo Indians into logical propositions. I can have impossible phenomena explained on my screen such as the congruence between left and right hands or movement on a Möbius strip. And I can play with all these things that have never existed before, with all these improbable possibilities, and in this way expand my universe.

Although this creative act of making the invisible visible and the unspeakable audible thrills me, I have still not yet come to the core of my universe. For I know that behind my terminal and the threads that stream from it sits still more. I know it because when I press a given key, messages from others appear, discs in the form of pictures that are addressed to me among others. And if I like, I can myself make the image from the other envisioner light up on the terminal—if I like, and if he likes. He can, if he likes, make this picture of mine light up on his terminal—if he likes, and if I like. We are aware of one other, and we agree dialogically. And *we* means, theoretically, "everyone."

Through this mutual recognition and acknowledgment of all others, my game with images takes on a very specific character, namely, that of a social game in which each of the changes I make to the image is at once an answer to a question that has been put to me and a challenge to all others to have further changes made and to be returned to me as a new question. In a highly responsible interaction, the main thing is not what is to be seen but from whom and to whom it is directed. I play with images not to exist in a particular way but rather to coexist.

All this proceeds at the speed of light. This means, on one hand, that everything appears only to instantly disappear and, on the other hand, that everything from a permanent memory rises only to sink back again, changed. The speed of light means that all time (past, present, future) coalesces at the moment it blazes up on the screen, at the point of "now." But at the same time, it means that all human beings, wherever they may be, are with me for the moment and that I myself can be everywhere in the world. The speed of light makes all space (reality, possibility, impossibility) coalesce on the screen's surface, at the point of "here." Everything is here and now, and I can change everything here and now. And all others are here and now with me. My universe is a concrete outside time and space, a point of creative coexistence with all others.

What I have tried to put into words here is both a feverishly involved and a passionate state of mind, something like a synthesis of what absorbs people in artistic and scientific creativity, in political activism, in revolutionary proclamations, in chess and roulette, in the stock market, and in libidinous dreams. It is a state of mind that does not intensify and then fall away, as in an orgasm, but that maintains itself at its orgiastic climax without interruption through a lifetime. For this state of mind is not physical but cerebral. Images are steering the telematic society in this direction: toward a continuous cerebral orgasm.

I admit, I am horrified now, as I come away from the emerging universe. Thank God I will not experience it. But I know that this horror should be resisted. It is the archaic horror of the mammalian human being that appears at each step away from mammalian essentials and toward greater cerebration. If I am able to overcome my horror, I can see what so repulsed me, namely, the pure aesthetic in the realm of images. All ethics, all ontology, all epistemology will be excluded from the pictures, and it will become meaningless to ask whether something is good or bad, real or artificial, true or false, or even what it means. The only remaining question is what I can experience (*aistheton,* "experience"). And with experiences, with the purely aesthetic, the distinction between action and passion, between doing something and tolerating it, falls away, for experience is both active and passionate. Cybernetic feedback between acting and being acted on characterizes experiences, and this feedback is the way the images exert control.

In modern languages, there is a sharp distinction between active and passive verb forms. "I care for sheep" and "sheep are cared for by me" present the same situation from opposite poles, and "sheep care for me" means a situation in which the elements are the reverse of what they were in the first sentence. In ancient Indo-Germanic and Semitic languages, however, there are forms (e.g., the Greek *aorist*), that might be expressed as "there is a caring for myself and for sheep." I conceive of images steering the telematic society toward this method and that, in the rising consciousness, the difference between active and passive will be suspended in favor of functional propositions.

A function $f(x, y)$ can, for example, be interpreted as follows: "camera and photographer are functions of photography." I suggest that the question, how will images govern in the telematic society? permits only this answer: images and society are functions of visualization. As I said earlier, the repulsive thing about this fair formulation is that all political categories are thrown out. In the emerging functional cybernetic level of consciousness, all historical, political thinking, beginning with Judeo-Christianity to Marxism and beyond, will be abandoned as unsuited to the telematic situation. For it will offer no means of deciding between acting and being acted on, between ruler and ruled, between those who govern and those who are governed. Everything there is a function of all other functions, so governing is a conjunction of all these functions. The brain can again serve as a model: in the brain, there is a cybernetic interplay among all cells and all the processes occurring between the cells. This is the way the brain governs us and the way we govern it.

To bring the situation existentially closer, I will replace the brain model with the model of an ant colony, for an ant colony can be considered a superbrain composed of single ant brains assembled like a mosaic. Because insects cannot attain the size of primates (as they grow, they must periodically shed their protective plates, and in this unshielded condition, the weight of a primate would crush them), they must form superbrains, such as ant colonies, to attain a brain size comparable to the human one. According to this model, the telematic society is a structure in which human brains follow the same cybernetic methods as ant brains. They function for one another, and function predominates.

But the ant metaphor (however fond cultural critics may be of it) has limits. For unlike the ant colony, the telematic society has no outside in which it could conceivably function. It is a global, universal society and therefore a self-contained one. Images are not its external but its internal secretions. What occurs in it are pure relationships, hallucinations, dreams of a global superbrain: pure aesthetics; art replacing politics, or art taking control.

All this has a cerebral character, the character of a cerebral orgasm. Just as for ants, everything is concentrated on the brain and antennae, and the rest of the body is only a kind of intestinal extension; for telematic people, everything will be focused on the brain and fingertips. And because everything is cerebral, it is characterized by an insatiable demand for new information, new adventures. Cerebral curiosity is insatiable. And the cerebral orgasm can, because it is hardly physical, never relax. This now needs to be investigated further.

To Shrink

Telematic society is a unique sort of ant colony: an ant colony because it has a mosaic-like structure in which all functions interact cybernetically, and unique because rather than working, a telematic ant will sit in its cell and spin apparitions, technical images, pure art. There will be brains that are linked through a dream-secreting superbrain to each other and to artificial brains. And yet there will be bodies attached, like anachronisms, to these brains, bodies that demand to be nourished, to reproduce, and to die: spoilsports.

These bodies, these spoilsports, these pretelematic participants in the telematic game must be pushed to the margins of view, behind the back of the player staring at the screen, because they cannot be completely eliminated. And this consideration for bodies, this regard for them, this looking back to pretelematic conditions will make them appear continually smaller, less interesting. They will shrink. Everything physical, everything voluminous is already beginning to atrophy, and I will examine this.

In the last stage of the modern era, there was a tendency to become outsized. Everything, from machines to empires, from sporting records to demands, grew into huge things. Now it is possible to recognize a reaction, a rising tendency toward the minute. It's something like a small mammal appearing to be a reaction against the giant dinosaurs. Even in late modernity, at the beginning of this century, tiny things—atoms, the quantum, calculus—became fascinating. In them, hopes rose and dangers lurked. It became clear that the concept of "enormity" (beyond human scale) applied not only to the very large but also to the small and that the nucleus of an atom can be more enormous than a galaxy. This reversal of attitude away from expansion and toward reduction can already be seen everywhere. "Small is beautiful" or "less is more" are slogans that articulate this reversal. And if we expect the world to end, then no longer as *tuba mirum spargit sonum*[1] but as "this is the way the world ends, not with a bang but a whimper."[2]

Everything seems to be getting smaller. Only the underdeveloped still want to grow, presumably to be able to shrink later. Devices, in particular, a central issue now, are becoming smaller, cheaper, and tend to shrink into invisibility and be delivered for free. The emerging telematic superbrain will be enormous because it will be a mosaic composed entirely of tiny stones.

For the moment, this shrinking of volumes is rationalized by way of the past, as a "crisis in growth," with arguments such as, say, the "exhaustion of oxygen and energy resources" or "protection of the environment." But it goes deeper. It is about a shift in existential interest that is already under way. Bodies are becoming steadily less interesting, and bodiless, insubstantial, immaterial information is becoming more and more interesting. And so the smaller a body is, the better. It doesn't get in the way so much; it can be overlooked. A personal computer is better than a Univac, an old beetle better than a new Audi, a shabby trailer home in Arizona better than a castle on the Loire, a fast-food lunch better than a ten-course meal. The less intrusive, the better. Everything large is intrusive and despised because it is large—large systems, in particular, including the panoramic view of future society proposed here. Telematic people, these antlike dwarfs, will find it disgusting.

(From this standpoint, incidentally, one gets a new insight into the victory of images over texts. In an image, infinitely many lines press into a surface so that small images can carry more information than thick books. Images beat texts because they are not so repulsive as massive rows of fat books.) So this text is directed not at telematic ants but at pretelematic mammals, first because it is panoramic and second because it is a text.

This contempt for size, for bodies, for one's own body has various sources. One is, as mentioned earlier, a reaction against the elephantiasis that came before. Giant monuments threatened to crush people. Another is the redundancy of "great people." A third comes up for discussion here, before we examine the root of the problem, namely, a fascination with minutiae. I mean the so-called sexual revolution or gender emancipation. It basically concerns a technology of releasing the libido from reproduction, freeing sex from biology. It involves not only birth control but also the automation of reproduction by means of sperm and egg banks and incubators. Orgasm is to be the only purpose for sexual intercourse. The first and harmless result is that women are free from the curse of having to bear children. But the second is the discovery, already in progress, that the site where orgasm is produced is not the sex organs but the brain. A truly free libido is one that is not only free from reproduction but from all things physical. This leads to contempt first for the sex of others and then for one's own sex and then to contempt for one's own body, as it appeared for the first time among the hippies and now appears everywhere in curious disguises. For example, the women's movement does not stand for a just division between the two sexes but for a contempt for sexual difference, and "black is beautiful" not for equality of all races but for contempt for all physical differences. In short, with a disdain for bodies, all biological criteria have lost interest.

Still, our current contempt for physical size, for bodies as such, for size as such, represents a regression, a distancing, an irony vis-à-vis all previous interests. Size and physicality have become ridiculous, unappetizing, unworthy (i.e., not worthy of interest). What is interesting now is the calculation and computation of minutiae to produce information. The vector of interest has been reversed.

Such reversals can be variously observed in the past. They are rare occurrences, and they lead to a transformation in existence as well as in the world where existence is. Ortega considers it to be the emergence of a new belief *(creencia),* and he distinguishes clearly between the field of interest (belief) that "has us" and the individual interests (ideas, opinions, knowledge, etc.) that "we have." I will give two examples of the reversal of the vector of interest in the past. In the second and third centuries, people began to despise those things that had previously interested them (e.g., the Roman Empire or Greek philosophy) and to be interested in something new. In Augustine's words, "*Deum atque animam cognoscere cupisco. Nihil-ne plus? Nihil*" (I want to know God and the soul. Nothing more? Nothing). What had previously been interesting had not disappeared from view. But it had shriveled and was absorbed and changed by a new field of interest. The empire became Christian, for example, and philosophy was subordinated to theology. The second example is that in the fifteenth century, people began suddenly to despise what had previously interested them (e.g., scholastic speculation) and to be interested in something new, namely, nature and spirit. In the words of Columbus, "*Gratias tibi ago, Domine, vidi rem novam*" (Thank God I have seen something new). It is not that the objects of earlier interest had disappeared from view; rather they shrank and were absorbed by a new field of interest. The scholastic universals debate, for example, was reworked into scientific theories of empirical and rationalistic perception, serving discovery and invention, technology that brought nature under the control of perceptive human beings.

I have given these examples to put the current reversal in the vector of interest (that which I have called elsewhere the "emergence of a new level of consciousness") into perspective. The new field of interest, this concentration on the infinitely small, on calculating and computing, is beginning to "have us." According to Ortega, it has become our belief. The science and technology in which we used to "believe," on the other hand, will no longer have us; rather we will have it. It will not disappear but will be absorbed by this new belief. We will make use of it in the service of our new belief. It will serve the needs of calculating and computing of the images in which we now believe (that now have us). In this sense, science and technology will existentially contract, even as they will undoubtedly expand exponentially as methods. They will be absorbed by new fields of interest. We will no longer be below science and technology (in "superstition"); rather science and technology will grow beneath us. From now on, superstition will be in images that will grow over us. This is how science and technology will change. They will be subordinate to the computation of images.

At the beginning of the essay, I spoke of the decay of lines into particles, of processes into quanta. I spoke, in Ortega's sense, of the decay of a belief. Now our interest is beginning to focus on points, while bodies and everything that has been abstracted from them (surfaces, lines) move toward the edge of our horizon of interest. We calculate and compute the points with the assistance of apparatuses to turn them into mosaic-like images. These images interest us. "*Nihil-ne plus? Nihil.*" A new imaginative force is appearing in and around us, and from it, in turn, the universe of technical images.

At the edge of this universe, this field of interest, everything from the past continues: science, technology, politics—in short, history. And many of us will continue to be interested in it for a long time. But from now on, this interest itself arises in the space of technical images, just as many remained interested in Christianity long after the Renaissance (and still today), and this interest changed completely in the space of the modern (e.g., the Reformation). Science, technology, politics (in short, history) will be so altered as to no longer deserve these names. They will serve the game of visionary power.

I will give an example of this contraction and change of science in the new field of interest, namely, the universe of discourse in physics. Once an infinite and eternal three-dimensional structure, in which bodies flowed along in linear time from the past into the future, which was likewise endless and eternal, this universe has shrunk to a kind of ephemeral balloon that is wrinkled in the fourth dimension, with wrinkles dense with possibilities. These possibilities can be grasped as an expanding, empty body. Such a universe has nothing concrete about it. It can be calculated and computed. And not only the universe, but also the discourse can be calculated and computed. There can be no believing in it, but given a capacity to imagine, one can play with it. The physical universe and the discourse of physics can be imagined as pictures on terminals.

This incipient disregard for bodies, including our own, this new regard for points, including our own fingertips, this transfer of our interest from stomachs and sex organs and volumes to conceptual antennae, this is the cerebral in the emerging society. At an earlier point in this essay, I used the image of a submarine breaking through an ice cover. The new interest—and with it the universe of technical images—is rising like an icebreaker, and everything that used to be interesting is gliding like bottom fish toward the horizon of interest. And so the visionary force that is emerging can be seen as a negation of everything that used to be interesting, as an ironic disregard of that formerly held in high regard. And if saying no is a sign of freedom, then one could maintain that the rising fortunes of things cerebral frees us from physicality.

Bodies denied in this way will, in fact, shrink and change but will not disappear. Human mammals will still need to be nourished, however minimally. They will also have to die, although perhaps differently from the way they do now (gradually, at an appointed time, and painlessly). They will therefore have to be reproduced as well, although perhaps also minimally. That is to say, even in the telematic society, there will have to be something like an economic infrastructure, for these bodies that cannot be completely ignored will have to have other bodies (e.g., nourishment) brought to them. The question of the economic structure of the emerging society is as interesting to us pretelematic mammals as it will be uninteresting for telematic people. For we see it as the question of corporeal suffering and death. For this reason, I plan to bracket out the question as it appears here and deal with it more closely in the next chapter. Here I would like to look again at the rejection of bodies and resulting shrinkage from the standpoint of saying no.

However human beings may define themselves in relation to other living things (whether as those that store acquired information, whether as those that oppose entropy, or whether as those that possess thought or spirit or soul), it is always as a life-form that tries to exceed its physical, organic, biological condition to become more cerebral, thinking, spiritual. It is, that is to say, a life-form that tries to neglect and devalue its own body and everything physical along with it. This rejection of everything physical, everything solid and substantial, is now at a new level. We are becoming less solid, and elements of our culture, too, are losing mass. The cult of slenderness, the nuclear family, pressure groups, terrorist cells, grills in the back garden, wind turbines instead of nuclear power plants, DIY in the tool shed could serve as examples. But it is important not to confuse this new level of rejection of things physical with the one that preceded it, namely, the Judeo-Christian rejection of the sensuous.

Judeo-Christian culture regarded the human body as a sinful vessel from which the soul was to be released and the world around us as a series of traps in which we are caught on our way to redemption. Judeo-Christianity therefore advises us to disregard what is "merely" physical. But we are standing at a higher level on the way to becoming cerebral. Bodies don't tempt us to become absorbed in them anymore; they bother us. We are already above them, and thanks to various disciplines (e.g., nuclear physics and cybernetics), we have learned that tiny bodies, purposefully manipulated, can be far more effective than giant ones. For example, a tiny quantity of enriched uranium can have a far greater effect than a million musk oxen, and a small group of terrorists with access to New York's power grid can have a greater effect on the American economy than a strike by millions. We have learned that the size of bodies is not a positive function—tiny causes can have vast effects—and that when it comes to bodies, mass is not necessarily an advantage. On the contrary, if bodies (our own and those in the outside world) are to be game tokens, they are more amusing if they're small. For example, pursuits that appear to pay homage to bodies (sunbathing, nude beaches, jogging, and bodybuilding) actually show contempt for them, degrading them to the level of a toy. And the smaller this toy body becomes, the less it disturbs the real game in which we are engaged, namely, a game with insubstantial information.

Looking toward the Far East, we could construct a pale picture of this world of rejected, contracted bodies in the land of dwarf trees, dwarf roosters, bound feet, portable kitchens, tiny ideograms, the minimal art of gray brush on transparent paper, the game of Go. It is also the land of chips, miniature apparatuses, and portable tomato cultures. The rejection of size and of the body is a cultural feature of the Far East, and it is no accident that the Romans called China the "land of gold-digging ants." Nor is it an accident that the telematic revolution in Japan took root so quickly. The rejection of the body found resonance not with the Judeo-Christian rejection of sensuality but rather with Confucian miniaturization. And when we talk about telematic society being "global," then we mean that it will be above all Chinese. For technical images can be regarded as a new form of ideogram, despite their formation in Western culture. With the loss of the alphabet, the West is dissolved in the East.

Telematic people will reject bodies: solids, objects, things. This means all telematic people, even those who currently seem uninterested in the play with pure information, wish to return to the physicality of organic sensations. All will feel the pull of tele-maticization, be drawn into its trajectory. Rejected, the objective world will blur on the horizon of telematic people. This world will become *unconditional,* in a sense of this word we do not yet grasp, and free in the way we say of the mind, that it goes where it will. It concerns a freedom like that brought about by drugs, a freedom to ignore the objective world, the world of conditions or things—a psychedelic freedom. Technical images are psychedelic.

The rejection of everything objective, tangible, physical is a rejection of all ontology, epistemology, and ethics in favor of a pure aesthetic. And this rejection is the value of the intellect. It is what Nietzsche meant when he said that "art is better than truth," in the land beyond good and evil. Whether this rejection is the same as that right of veto I discussed earlier, however, is another question.

To Suffer

The following considerations regarding the so-called economic infrastructure of the emerging society rely on a social model, namely, that of Platonic utopia, slightly adjusted. According to Plato, we are beings who have fallen from heaven *(topos uranikos)* into the world of appearances *(phainomena).* At home in heaven, we saw eternal and durable ideas in their logical order. Falling into the world, we were engulfed in the river of forgetting (Lethe), and its waters washed away all memory of the Ideas. We have forgotten them. So we come into the world as beings without ideas (idiots), and we can live out an entire idiotic life in the world, turning in circles, for example, cooking to eat and eating to cook, or sowing to reap and reaping to sow, or working to rest and resting to work—fundamentally, living to die and dying to be reborn in our children. This self-motivated idiotic life follows the order of a kitchen *(oikonomia),* and Plato also calls it *zoon oikonomikon:* the economic life—in the sense that *Wirtschaft* (economy) in German means a restaurant.

Yet there are methods we can use to remember the Ideas, for example, the idea of a jug, the "jugness" we beheld in heaven. And should we do this, we can impress this idea on a phenomenon, for example, on formless clay, to bring the phenomenal world into accord with the ideal world. The result, an earthly jug, will then be our work. And as soon as the jug has been made, we can set it outside the kitchen door, publicize it, politicize it, to exchange it for the work of another and thereby establish its value. This working and publicizing life Plato calls *bios politicos:* life directed toward the marketplace.

But as we look at the jug, we see that the idea of jugness has been distorted by the clay. It is no longer so perfect as it was in heaven, and anyone who believes in such phenomenal ideas will have only distorted ideas (*doxai,* "opinions"). Political life is therefore a life of false opinions, orthodoxies, paradoxes, heterodoxes—in short, errors. We can avoid this error only by comparing the jug with jugness, by criticizing it. This requires us to turn our attention to jugness and all other heavenly ideas: *theoria.* Meanwhile, we are standing in the middle of the marketplace with works all around us, gazing upward. Plato calls this observing life, back turned to phenomena, *bios philosophikos:* life in the love of wisdom.

In utopia, these three forms of life—economy, politics, and philosophy—form a stepladder. The economy supports politics because without economic support, a craftsman would not have the leisure to make a jug. Politics supports philosophy because without the marketplace and the works set out there, a philosopher could not compare (criticize) and steer *(kybernein)* the establishment of values. Idiots, slaves (the economy), are society's base; its middle ground are artists and publicists (politics); and theorists, those who steer (philosophy), are the kings. The purpose of the republic *(politeia)* is to open a space for philosophy, for remembering and unforgetting ideas (*aletheia* = un-forget, "truth"), and so to return to our heavenly home.

The key word in the social model is leisure (Greek: *schole;* Latin: *otium*), and its opposite, business (Greek: *a-scholia;* Latin: *negotium*). Slaves of the economic life are always occupied, busy, economically engaged, even when they are sleeping, for they are then preparing themselves for business to come. Artists of the political life enjoy leisure (have a break, criticize their works, reflect on ideas) when they have completed a work. They "go to school" periodically. Theoreticians of the philosophical life live in leisure, in school. The purpose of the republic is to permit an elite to live in school to make a return to a heavenly home available to all.

This utopian social model was the ideal of feudalism. There the peasants lived in the economy, the townsmen in the workshop, and the monks in school to open the way for a return to heaven. With the bourgeois revolution of the fifteenth century, the workshop set itself above the school, and theories needed to serve the needs of manufacture. Bourgeois society no longer sought wisdom at leisure but rather to change the world through progress. With the Industrial Revolution of the nineteenth century, the economy set itself above the workshop. Industrial society no longer sought world change but rather ever-increasing consumption, occupation, business. Slaves, apparently freed, became kings, and the way back to heaven closed.

I will now try to apply this model to the present essay. In "To Prepare," I described the telematic society as a school in which everyone lives all the time. In "To Govern," I described the telematic society as one governed automatically, in which it is meaningless to speak of politics. Have I then already taken the telematic society to be a realization of a Platonic utopia, that is, as a society in which slaves (economy) are robots, artists (politics) are automatic intelligences, in which everyone lives for theory (all are philosophers, kings), nourished and supplied with criticizable models by robots and artificial intelligences? Is cybernetic society a structure in which everyone lives at leisure and where all work (economy) and all effects (politics) become subhuman? Basically, is a situation in which everyone contemplates images (whether it be to receive, to change, or to forward them on), and in which the cycle of the economy and the process of production takes place behind people's backs, the very situation that Plato called life in the love of wisdom?

The answer to this is regrettably sobering. For as long as human mammals depend on the brains and fingertips of future telematic people (i.e., in the foreseeable future), it will remain impossible to ignore the economy, to philosophize, to have leisure, to live in school. And this is not primarily because mammals must be nourished and reproduced—this task could in fact be taken over by automata—but primarily because mammals suffer and die. And this shows what the economy is about and what we are sometimes in danger of forgetting: about suffering and about death.

An economy is accordingly not so much a method of preserving and reproducing human bodies but of ameliorating their suffering (that which Buddhism calls their "thirst") and postponing their death. Economics and medicine are fundamentally synonyms.

I won't speak here of death. For this whole essay, which appears to be about the emerging universe of technical images, is, in fact, an effort to become immortal through images. Memory, the opposite of death, is the theme (and the motive) of this effort (i.e., of this essay as well as of telematics). But death and dying are not the same. Dying means to suffer death. So in keeping with the reflections introduced earlier, dying belongs in the realm of the economic. Without doing violence to Plato, the matter can be formulated as follows: economics is the field of dying, politics the field of not wanting to die, and philosophy the field of immortality. And this means that in this chapter on the future economy, I am not obliged to speak of death, that I can restrict myself to speaking of suffering. For dying is contained in the nature of suffering: whatever I suffer from (even if it be a toothache), I have a foretaste of dying, and one can assume that in dying, all suffering is concentrated on death, that it only then deserves to be called suffering.

The economy is a method of providing bodies with the means of not suffering (dying). Consider, for example, food. In places where the economy functions poorly, for example, in the third world, people suffer. It is incidentally becoming increasingly clear that the economy is a medical problem and medicine an economic one. To gain insight into this, it is enough to see the distended bellies of third-world children who are the victims of drought. Because the human body is a solid, the economic and medical means (essentials such as meat or aspirin) are bodies as well. They are objects informed with the purpose of ameliorating suffering. Robots can inform objects (work) as well as deliver informed objects to human bodies (distribution). Robots can act and exchange. In this sense, human beings will be shut out of the economy: production as well as distribution of goods will be done automatically, behind the backs of people watching images (in the machinery of the telematic ant colony).

The reproduction of bodies, too, is an economic issue. It, too, serves to defer dying (of the species, not the individual body). And because it likewise involves bodies, it, too, can be done by robots. Behind the backs of people watching images, robots can take sperm and egg to incubate new watchers of images. Only then will the libido be capable of true cerebration. So even in this aspect of physiology, of the economy, human beings will become superfluous.

But robots cannot do our suffering for us. And this is not, as one might think, because there are no methods of turning away from suffering. One need only think back to the Stoics and Epicurus to see such methods. Only such methods cannot be integrated (or only very indirectly) with the process of automation. For in the end, they all rest on the possibility of suicide to avoid pain. If we take Schopenhauer (of whom I intend to speak further) to assist as a witness, we would recognize suffering and living as synonyms. As long as we have bodies, suffering (and with it, the economy) will form the base of society. And this is not for physiological but for existential reasons. For pain can be relieved, suffering can be numbed. But as soon as the body is anaesthetized, consciousness becomes quiet and numb: an-aesthetic. Consciousness, to be consciousness at all, is an unhappy consciousness. If all pain were relieved, all suffering numbed, the economy would be superseded. We could turn our backs to it and practice philosophy. But then there would be nothing left over which to philosophize. The Platonic social model, applied to telematics, shows that the Platonic utopia (in fact, any utopia) hides an internal contradiction: there can be no happiness without suffering. Utopia is impossible.

So the economy will continue to form the base of the society of technical images, but it will have changed so completely from the present one that our current models (whether they be liberal or Marxist or whatever) will miss the mark. For a telematic economy will not be about coveted goods but about necessary evil. Economic activity will no longer be regarded as a way of life but as an interruption of learning. Such contempt and fear of things economic may be reminiscent of Platonic aristocracy (of aristocracy in general) and, in fact, all human beings will be aristocrats in relation to the working robots. And yet categories other than the Platonic (and aristocratic in general) will be needed to grasp the economic base. I would like to focus on two categories, namely, "perception," the seat of suffering in the brain, and the unique category "sympathy."

The greatest scandal of the present day is medicine. It is scandalous not because it functions scandalously (see the third world) but because it rests on scandalous assumptions. Above all is the assumption that the living body is property and that it ought to be kept alive. In the near future, it will probably become incomprehensible that such a scandal could have been tolerated. Of course, the explanation is simple. If cultural objects are regarded as property to be used, then the living body is the greatest property of all, the focus of all others. Medicine today is nothing but the central point of today's economy. But the moment this interest shifts from cultural objects to pure information (to technical images), contemporary medicine will be revealed as a crime against human dignity. As long as some bit of brain remains in the living body, something that cannot be made completely robotic, the body continues to be a necessary evil. The body should disturb play (living) as little as possible, be a spoilsport as little as possible. And when this is no longer possible, when the body puts defects into play that cannot be repaired, medicine has the task of removing it with as little intrusion as possible.

Medicine (economy) should be the means of alleviating suffering when it does so to delay death and where the suffering cannot be alleviated, to remove the body. In a dialogically ordered society, death could no longer be distinguished from suicide: the decision to put a suffering body down—euthanasia—would be made in dialogue (e.g., between a doctor and the one who is suffering).

I chose the example of medicine not only because it is so striking but above all because it emphasizes the cerebral nature of suffering. As long as corporeal processes (or economic processes of any sort) do not enter into consciousness, as long as they proceed automatically, they can and should be ignored. To become interested in one's own liver function, or in one's morning toast, is to miss a chance to produce pictures. Should there be a programming error (the liver is forcing itself into consciousness by being painful or the burned toast by tasting terrible), one would feel obliged to reprogram, in cooperation with others. And when it becomes clear that such reprogramming is getting on people's nerves (especially those nerves engaged in making pictures), there is an option to say no, to exercise one's veto option and forget everything (die). For one will not be forgotten: artificial memories see to it that what was once called the "I" is stored so that it can be dialogically changed. So that is the economy: an evil that is necessary in order not to be forgotten. It is, nonetheless, an evil that can be forgotten by the one who decides to say no. The only one who can afford to despise the economy is the one who exercises the freedom of the veto.

Unfortunately, one must take an interest in the economy (including one's own body) when programs are faulty, when one becomes aware of suffering. This awareness is, however, dialogically ordered. When one of the knots in the net (a single "I") becomes aware of suffering, the entire net becomes sympathetic. If the economy has to become interesting, if it has to manifest the impossibility of reducing it to a robotic substructure, this will be as a result of sympathy. Telematic society will be concerned with poorly programmed bodies (livers, loaves) out of sympathy to reprogram them and finally to be able to ignore them.

All consciousness is an unhappy consciousness, even that emerging awareness of a visionary power that is about to give rise to the universe of technical images. The source of all creativity is suffering. In pretelematic times, this suffering was primarily something individual, private. An entire literature is devoted to this creative suffering. In a telematic situation, the source of creativity is sympathy. One could call it love, if one so desired. But a better way might be to perceive others' suffering (and dying) by recognizing one's own suffering (and dying). So the following watch phrase might be set over the telematic society: *I am mortal, you are mortal, we are mortal.* This would be an approximate formulation of telematics's negatively entropic project.

In summary, something like the following can be predicted about the economic infrastructure of the coming society: action and trade will be largely automated and will not be interesting. The objects produced and consumed there will not impinge on a consciousness absorbed in images. People will neither work nor make works, and in this sense, society will approach a Platonic utopia. All will become kings, all will live in school (leisure) and will become philosophers. And yet occasionally, something will malfunction. Accidents will happen. People will suffer (and die). These accidents will impinge on consciousness and will be interesting. Because there must be such accidents (predictable, unsurprising, redundant), every effort will be made to keep them at a minimum. Better and better methods will probably have been worked out: suffering will occur more rarely and death later. But even the increasing rarity can be calculated. When repairs become too expensive, when they disturb life in school, when they spoil the pleasure of the game, the disturbance will be forgotten. This, I think, is how all dying will be in the future: a dialogically negotiated agreement to forget.

Economic sciences will be grouped together as those disciplines that quantify values. I hope that these prophetic reflections will provoke discussion of the coming reordering of all values. In any case, that was, I confess, their real intention.

To Celebrate

In the Platonic model I discussed briefly in the previous chapter, a high priority is placed on leisure *(schole)*. It is the goal of life, the seat of wisdom. And it looks as though we are approaching this goal with seven-mile boots. Unemployment is spreading, and automata are taking over those gestures instituted by human beings to change the environment. The division of labor is gradually becoming a question asked by robots of programmers, less a political than a mathematical question. The matter of leisure, so readily dismissed today with the notion of "managing free time," therefore presents an ever more urgent question. If the previous chapter has been remotely successful in its estimate of the coming telematic society, there can be no doubt that the question of leisure must stand at the center of this entire essay.

It is not only about quantities, not only about how more and more free time ought to be apportioned. In fact, the time between shifts for the politically conscious craftsman has turned into the holidays, leave, and pensions of the economically conscious industrial worker, and again into the cybernetic life of the information-consuming functionary, only periodically interrupted by work. Quantitatively, then, the relationship between work and leisure has reversed itself so that instead of holidays, one ought to speak of service days. In the telematic society, free time is all there is to be discussed. Nevertheless, it is not so much the division of leisure time into hours, days, or years that is at stake but the experience of leisure, of enjoyment. Telematic society should live pleasurably, should exploit its own imaginative capacities.

We can better approach enjoyment by temporarily forgetting the Platonic concept of leisure as the seat of wisdom, the theoretical life, and turn our attention to the other root of our culture, namely, Judaism. There we encounter the Sabbath. It is holy, the only thing that is, in fact, apart from God himself; the commandment says, "Thou shalt observe the Sabbath, to keep it holy." This is, however, a holiness Plato would not have understood. For him, as for our entire Greek tradition, holiness is detached and protected from the space of the polis. It is a *temenos,* a temple, a place of observation, leisure—a school, in fact. It is a refuge under the protection of a god, such as the god Akademos, where one goes to exchange ideas with other leisured beings. The Sabbath, by contrast, is a space held above and apart from the flow of events, a temple not of marble but of time, and it is therefore only holy when someone separates it from history, when someone celebrates it.

By lifting the Sabbath out of linear time (out of the week), history is interrupted. The six days of the week then flow into the Sabbath, where they are lifted. History happens during the six days of the week (God creates the world) so as not to do anything on the Sabbath (nothing happens; God rests). The six days of the week pursue a goal—they are motivated, they intend something. Their goal, their motive, their intention (the goal, motive, intention of any history whatsoever) is the Sabbath. The Sabbath itself, meanwhile, stands still—it has no goal, no motive, no intention, for it is itself the goal, the motive. The six days of the week are meaning-full, and their meaning is the Sabbath. The Sabbath itself, by contrast, is meaningless exactly because it is itself the meaning. The six days of the week are value-able, and their value is the Sabbath. The Sabbath itself, on the other hand, has no value because it is itself the value. This is why the Sabbath, if it is kept, is holy. It transcends history. A kabbalistic interpretation of messianic time reads that it is that time when two Sabbaths follow one another with nothing in between. And for Christianity, it is the holy moment of the

Sabbath between Good Friday and Easter Sunday. Here history is suspended. It is the joyous moment of redemption from suffering.

Not that the Judeo-Christian concept of joy, of holiness, is opposed to the Greek concept of theory, contemplation, philosophy. Both stand for a transcending of history, for posthistory. In both cases, the academy and the celebration of Sabbath, one turns one's back to the economy and rises to that which was called, in Faust, "The Mothers."[1] Still there is a crucial difference between an academic and a celebratory life. For in the academy, one looks (one sees ideas there), and in celebration, one listens (one is called). The academy is a segment of space. There one sees forms. The Sabbath celebration is a segment of time, and there one gains a calling. This is why Greek leisure is contemplation, and the joyous leisure of Judeo-Christianity is responsibility (response to a call). Greek leisure is essential, where essences are to be seen. Joyous leisure is by contrast existential, where something categorically "other" is to be encountered. In Greek leisure, one discovers the holy (*aletheia* = discovery, "truth"). In celebratory leisure, the holy makes itself manifest, has its say. Only when leisure and celebration meet, when the academy blends with the Sabbath, when space and time are mutually suspended, could it be said that the Western tradition has reached completion. This is the religious aspect of telematics.

Since the bourgeois revolution of the fifteenth century, we have forgotten how to celebrate. In history books, this forgetting is usually referred to as "modern life becoming profane." According to the Platonic model sketched in the previous chapter, theory was subordinated to practice from the time of the bourgeois revolution: from this point, theoretical leisure served the interests of progressive world change. From the Judeo-Christian standpoint, the bourgeois revolution repressed celebration in the interests of utility. The leisure of holidays would henceforth serve as a time of recovery for the useful activity that would follow; academy and Sabbath would be subordinated to work (to technology, to the working day). The

Industrial Revolution of the nineteenth century completed this secularization of the school and celebration. Theory itself became a technology, an enterprise involving institutions built and financed expressly for this purpose. Celebration became a weekend, a summer vacation, or a ski trip, organized by institutions specializing in such things. In this way, the bourgeois revolution integrated leisure, both in its Greek and in its Judeo-Christian senses, into labor, and the Industrial Revolution in its turn built this leisure-fed labor into the industrial economy.

In an odd way, the automation revolution we are now experiencing exposes this integration of leisure into labor and the following integration of labor into the economy. For it shows that a degraded and secularized leisure is swelling up inside labor and that as labor is digested by the economy, the whole industrial economy blows up like a soap bubble. This is why the current problem of leisure activity, unemployment, and free time is first and foremost an economic problem. It puts industry and industriousness into question. From the standpoint of industry, the problem of increasing leisure presents a political problem. For thanks to automation, leisure is no longer the root of all evil but, on the contrary, the reward for all virtue. A leisure that gains the upper hand represents the antithesis of business and, furthermore, the antithesis of bourgeois values. But both the economic and the political view of work displaced by leisure deflect attention from the actual problem: that we don't know how to be idle; we don't know how to celebrate.

Our incapacity to celebrate can be observed in the way we use the word *idle*. We use it in passing, with a dismissive gesture, for example, when we say it's idle to speculate about something. *Idle* clearly means "pointless." But the ancient Greeks knew that *pointless* is a synonym for *pure*. They knew that philosophy depends on idle speculation about something. And the ancient Jews kept the Sabbath holy expressly to keep it distinct from the working day, to be able to speculate idly about holy texts for that length of time. For both these prebourgeois traditions, *idle* is an expression for the human capacity to rise above the purposeful. It is a celebratory expression. And unless we can remember the meaning of the word, we will remain incapable of recognizing unemployment as a blessing.

One way of remembering is to observe the difference between human and animal gestures. Human beings do make purposeful (economic) gestures: like any other animal, they reach for things to eat and things with which to copulate, and they hold dangerous things at bay. But purposeless, useless, antieconomic, celebratory gestures may be observed as well. Children play with inedible, infertile, harmless pebbles, for example; they play theoretically. It says something about our obliviousness of the sacred status of leisure that we interpret such games as utilitarian and say, for example, that a useful object such as a stone knife, a culture of use, arose from such a pebble game. In this way, we lose sight of the cultural centrality of uselessness and leisure, the festive and theoretical, that is to say, art and theoretical science. A phenomenology of human gestures can remind us that humans are festive beings, religious in the Judeo-Christian sense.

This is basically the message of the religious tradition, to remind us of the purposelessness, the festivity of human life. But we have become deaf to this message, unless, perhaps, it comes to us through the filter of a more accessible discourse, for example, through Kierkegaard. His work goes to some length to show the power of "religious life" (a life before God, without purpose) over "ethical life" (a purposeful life in politics and commerce). One of the basic themes of this essay is that we now have a new and unexpected method of regaining Kierkegaard's insight into religious life. That is telematics, which permits us to recognize ourselves in others through images festively, leisurely, without purpose.

It therefore seems completely wrong of me to wonder to what purpose people will make images in the future. Such a question is typical of pretelematic, historical, purpose-bound thinking. If my predictions are accurate, the state of mind of people of the future will be precisely the relaxation of making images, beyond any what for, in the absence of motive. They will live without problems, no longer butting up against objects and obstacles but in pure education, at leisure. Everything they do will be relaxed; they will live in celebration. One giant Sabbath will engulf future humanity. And if that seems endlessly boring, it is because we, despite all our festivals (or perhaps exactly because of them), have forgotten what *celebrate* means.

In the chapter "To Play," I was trying to say the same thing. There, however, I approached the matter from the profane side. "Playing" and "celebrating" are in fact related concepts. This can be seen, as I said, in the celebratory gestures of children as they play, except that games can be won or lost, and in celebrating, there is nothing to win. In contrast to all other societies, the telematic society will produce no winnings from its play. New information will be generated continually, the sum of available information will continually grow larger, but this flow of information will not become useful, will not become profit. It will only be celebrated.

In the religious atmosphere of this chapter, the question of programming can be asked afresh. What do I actually mean when I say of telematics that it permits a dialogical programming of image-producing apparatuses? For one thing, I certainly mean that there will be no centralized senders but that each image maker, sitting before his terminal, will be able to program his own apparatus. I mean that all these individual programs will be measured against one another, enriching and correcting one another, and that there will be an ongoing dialogical programming of all apparatuses by all participants; that people of the future will be distinguishable from the functionaries of today in that unlike functionaries, they will program rather than be programmed. But by dialogical programming, I mean, in consideration of celebration and festivity, something far more basic. I mean roughly that which Buber called "dialogic life."

In the concept of "self-programming" under discussion here, the stress lies on "self." It is my program and no one else's. I want to have my program so that I won't be subject to anyone else's. I want to possess not to be possessed. Elsewhere, this essay was concerned with "ownership" and "possession" as categories that would no longer apply to the information society. In this context, the concept of "self-programming" would have no meaning. Yet this contradicts the experience we currently have of the emerging society. We experience it as an imperialism of information. Senders possess the programs, and we are possessed by them. To make a program telematic would therefore be to extract it from the possession of the sender to make it the possession of all participants. In the current state of affairs, therefore, *self-programming* might rather mean "dispossession," the socialization of imperialistic programs. It is a socializing term.

Once the telematic society really arrives, however, the concept "self-program" won't be able to sustain this meaning. Once the centralized senders are gone, dispossession will no longer be relevant. Only dialogical programming will be relevant. Then there will be no point in having one's own program so that it cannot be displaced by another's. On the contrary, the point will be to have other programs (programs of others) to be able to change them (to suggest them to others). So when there really is a telematic society, rather than our own programs, we will be discussing *alternative programs,* a neologism that strikes me as characteristic of telematic society.

These considerations bring us to the paired concepts of my own and another's, concepts that carry a heavy load. To try to unburden it (as Heidegger did in *Identity and Difference* and as the debate between Sartre and Foucault tried to do) is to recognize the reversibility of the terms. One's own is what is not another's. To identify $(a = a)$ is to define difference in relation to another $(a = \sim[\sim a])$. Understanding this, not only logically but existentially, breaks open the shell that encapsulates me, what is uniquely mine, what

I possess, leaving an open view of what is absolutely other. "I" then becomes something that is the other of the absolute other.

Judaism forbade the making of images, and Christianity and Islam, each in its own way, have followed the same path. This is because images made by human beings obscure the "true image." The "true image" is any human face. It is the image of the absolute other, the "likeness of God." Each human being is, for me, the likeness of God, and "I" am the likeness of God for all others. Therefore each human being is the other for me, and I am the other for all human beings, an image of the "absolute other" (God). Because each person is for me the true image of the absolute other, he is the only image, the only way I can or should conceive of God. All other images I make of God or anything else are false images and so forbidden. Every single person is my only medium to God, and I can only come to God if I go to Him through the other (each other one). All other media (all other images, representations, and ideas) are false media. They are idolatrous. The only true love of God is love of another, human love. So "thou shalt love thy God [the absolute other] with all thy heart, and all thy soul, and everything that thou hast" is synonymous with "love thy neighbor [another]."

All pretelematic images, from Lascaux to video, are discursive, broadcast images, projected against the other, obscuring his face. They are forbidden. They lead the wrong way, away from God. Telematic, dialogically synthesized images, on the other hand, are media between one human being and another, through which I may see the face of the other. And through this face I may see God. Dialogical programming of images (the dialogical life) can therefore be a celebration of God (of the absolute other), each one with all others and by means of all others, a prayer. That is basically what I meant by alternative programs.

We may be at the point of remembering how to celebrate. We may be at the point of finding our way back, on a strange detour through telematics, to being genuinely human, that is, to a festive existence for another, to purposeless play with others and for others. Even now, we are beginning to be repulsed by pretelematic existence, an existence bound up with purpose and motives, always harping away at what is one's own, as a frightfully serious, joyless, and so profane way of life. A new, completely unorthodox religiosity is beginning to emerge from the musty corners of our consciousness, and this, surprisingly, in the form of the dreamlike universe of technical images.

Chamber Music

The titles of all previous chapters are verbs, in fact, infinitives, calling attention to the way these thoughts push outward, never reaching the horizon. The title of this penultimate chapter is a substantive, to express the hope that the thoughts have arrived at something substantial. This tension between the unbounded quality of the infinitive and the definability of the substantive characterizes not only this essay but any kind of forecasting.

Forecasting is not a matter of seeing what's coming. A forecaster looks in the direction in which the present seems to be pointing, at how things will come out, not at what is coming. One can predict outcomes but not what is to come. A forecaster covers up the future with outcomes so that there is no future. He anticipates the future with information to avert the future. The Heideggerian concept of "precaution" expresses it. To take a precaution is not only to concern oneself with a particular possibility but also to provide for this possibility, to draw it into the present, anticipate it to do away with it. All prediction damages the future. This can be observed on computer screens. Developments, tendencies, curves can be projected from the present forward, and these projections can be manipulated. Margins of error can be calculated as closely as one likes. But such projections show the results of calculations, not what is coming. There is no future. Computerized prediction devours the future in the interest of avoiding catastrophe.

But catastrophes cannot be avoided because they cannot be foreseen. Whatever I may foresee is by definition not a catastrophe.

I can project scenarios to undermine my expectations for a telematic society—a nuclear war, for example, or a third-world revolt, or, more interestingly, the decay of a system as complex and vulnerable as a dialogically ordered society would have to be. I can project a scenario in which the repressed physicality of the telematic society would reassert itself against the tendency to become more and more cerebral, producing an unprecedented level of bestiality. But such scenarios do not describe catastrophes: they describe things that are predictable and that therefore can, at least theoretically, be avoided.

True catastrophes cannot be foreseen. They are emergencies. For example, if I am throwing stones at a windowpane with increasing force, I can calculate the change in the angle of reflection each stone makes as it falls back from the window, order them into a curve, and project this curve. I will reach the point at which the window breaks. That is a true catastrophe, for I cannot extend my curve to predict the trajectory of the stone on the other side of the window. To do this, I would have to have information that is not available on this side of the window. True catastrophes are new information. They are, by definition, surprising adventures. In this essay, I have proposed that human engagement consists in bringing about surprising adventures, catastrophes, and that telematics realizes this engagement, theoretically and technically. Telematic society is, then, a structure for realizing catastrophes. Therefore any attempt to predict it, as I have done here, is contradictory and self-referential—Ouroboros, the snake that swallows its own tail.

There is also another reason that what I tried to do here was impossible. I took certain contemporary tendencies as my starting points, for example, the tendency of technical images to become more and more immediate and to repress texts or the tendency of images to become electronic or the tendency of apparatuses to become smaller and cheaper and to penetrate into the smallest spaces. I did not invent these tendencies; I discovered them. But an infinity of tendencies stream from every phenomenon, surrounding it with a cloud of futures. That is exactly what makes a phenomenon concrete, that it is a core surrounded by innumerable possibilities. I selected several of these possibilities and neglected all the others, using probability as my criterion: the neglected possibilities seemed improbable. But this criterion contradicts everything this essay has tried to say: that we are interested in precisely what is improbable. And so to the extent this essay predicts anything, it contradicts its own premises.

And yet both are impossible: to predict and not to predict. This is one of the contradictions that characterizes human existence, and what I've tried to say here acknowledges this contradiction. In other words, telematic society, as I foresee it here, is not what is approaching but what we worry about because it is emerging from us. This is not the music of the future but rather a critique of the present.

The scenario, the fable, I propose here is this: people will sit in separate cells, playing with their fingertips on keyboards, staring at tiny screens, receiving, changing, and sending images. Behind their backs, robots will bring them things to maintain and reproduce their derelict bodies. People will be in contact with one another through their fingertips and so form a dialogical net, a global superbrain, whose function will be to calculate and compute improbable situations into pictures, to bring information, catastrophes about. Artificial intelligences will also be in dialogue with human beings, connected through cables and similar nerve strands. In terms of function, then, it will be meaningless to try to distinguish between natural and artificial intelligences (between primate brains and secondary brains). The whole thing will function as a cybernetically controlled system that cannot be divided into constituent elements: a black box.

The prevailing state of mind will be reminiscent of the one we experience in our creative moments, the experience of being out of oneself, of adventure, of orgasm. The telematic superbrain will radiate an ever-expanding, self-renewing, and self-concentrating

aura of technical images. It will present a universal spectacle, although a modest rather than a grand one. For the emissions of the
superbrain will not be directed outward into the void but inward,
toward endless tiny terminals. It will be a mosaic spectacle, a game
with tiny pieces. The superbrain will play internally, it will dream—
a universal spectacle as a montage game of tiny parts, a black box
composed entirely of darkened rooms, a universal orchestra made
up entirely of chamber musicians.

This brings us to a closer examination of chamber music—not
the sort one hears in concern halls but the sort experienced by those
who meet to make music. I imagine these musicians meeting not to
read scores but to improvise from available scores, as was common
in the Renaissance. A recording of the music will become the basis
for further improvisation by future musicians. This is to suggest
chamber music as a model for dialogic communication in general,
and for telematic communication in particular.

The basis for such music making is an original score, a program,
a set of rules. But using recordings of recordings of recordings,
this score will soon disappear behind the horizon of musicians
who are improvising with continually reprogrammed memories.
In chamber music, there is no director, no government. The one
who sets the tempo is only temporarily directing things. And
yet chamber music demands an exceptionally close adherence
to rules. It is cybernetic. Chamber music is pure play, by and for
the players, for whom listeners are superfluous and intrusive. It
employs participation (strategy) rather than observation (theory).
Precisely to play as though it were playing solo, each instrument
plays as though it were an accompaniment. To play for himself,
each player plays for all the others. Each improvises together with
all the others, which is to say, each adheres to precise rules (consensus) to jointly change them in the course of the playing. Each
player is both a sender and a receiver of information. His goal is to
synthesize new information to become more than the playing. This
information is pure, with no tangible substrate, except, of course,

for the recording device. But this recording device is nothing like the work of chamber music (the result of the work); rather it serves as its memory, which is durable and can be randomly replayed. It is futile to look for the meaning of the information that emerges in this way anywhere but in the game itself, in the players and the rules they follow.

In short, chamber music can serve as a model of telematic social structure. In itself, it precedes telematics, the apparatus, and automation. It is a preindustrial form of communication. And yet it is now possible to see in it (and perhaps in jazz, so strongly reminiscent of chamber music) many aspects of postindustrial communication, above all the camera obscura aspect. This may, incidentally, explain the otherwise remarkable contemporary interest in chamber music (and jazz): we recognize in it the form of a future society.

And yet there are divergences as well as parallels between the structure of chamber music and that of the emerging telematic society. Whereas classical scores have blank spots that challenge players to improvise, programs are in themselves challenges to improvise. In this sense, many modern scores should be called "programs." So what the recording device is for chamber music, artificial memories are for telematics, although in contrast to the recorder, the intelligences participate actively in the dialogue so that in them, past, present, and future converge. The essential difference between chamber music and telematics is therefore as follows: chamber music takes place in linear time, develops themes, and one improvisation follows another. Telematics, on the other hand, occurs in a simultaneous time and space, and all players in all places make decisions relating to themes and their variations all at once. That is the difference between pressing on a piano key and on the key of the apparatus.

Despite this difference, the comparison between chamber music and telematics occurred to me long ago, long before I began to write this essay. Had I proposed this comparison at an earlier point in my thinking, I would have made it easier to gain an insight into telematics. Unfortunately, I felt forced to defer the model until now because it comes from the world of music. As the reader will surely have realized with surprise and annoyance, I have excluded everything to do with ear and mouth, with sound and words, from my thinking. I have omitted the audiovisual character of the universe of technical images. For I am convinced that only now has the moment come to speak about this. My conviction about this is one of the motivations for this work.

The universe of music is, according to Schopenhauer, the "world as will." It doesn't represent anything. Schopenhauer sets this universe in contrast to the "world as representation," the universe of technical images. The universe of music is not grounded in anyone's imagination but in some sort of biological drive. Musical information does not depend on the receiver's ability to decode it (such as an ear linked to a brain); rather it permeates the receiver's body with vibrations, which bring this body into resonance (sympathy). The universe of technical images, on the other hand, emerges from the imagination, from a kind of intellect. It presents something and wants to be deciphered. And so the universe of technical images (the world as representation) sets itself before the universe of music (before the world as will) and covers it like a veil. In other words, the world of music is concrete life (will and suffering), and the world of images is abstract conjuring, "Maya." I will now argue against Schopenhauer.

The world of music is a composed universe. *Compose* and *compute* are synonyms. We don't need to wait for electronic music to recognize this quality about music: the universe of music is as calculated and computed as that of technical images. It is true that technical images are calculated and computed representations and belong in this sense to Schopenhauer's world as representation. But as I tried to show in the suggested model, the universe of technical images is reminiscent of many things about the musical universe. In contrast to the musical one, it is a universe of surfaces, but like the musical one, it is a pure universe, free of any semantic dimension.

Technical images are pure art in the same sense that music alone once was. And so one can say that with the rise of technical images, a new level of consciousness is reached, namely, one that makes music with visionary power.

This, I think, is the only way the audiovisual character of the universe of technical images can be understood. Since the beginning of computing, technical images have rushed spontaneously to sound, and from sound spontaneously to images, binding them. To look at it another way, all pretechnical images and all pretechnical music could be understood as aspiring to technical sounding images, making the technical image the first instance of music becoming an image and an image becoming music. There are, in fact, contemporary devices that automatically translate image into sound and sound into images (electronic mixers), but this is exactly what is not meant here. In a sounding image, the image does not mix with music; rather both are raised to a new level, the audiovisual, which could not realize its meaning until now because of its grounding in earlier levels.

Contemporary approaches to making music pictorial and pictures musical have had a long preparation. They can be seen, for example, in so-called abstract painting and in the scores of newer musical compositions. But only synthesized images are really conceived musically and made musical with visualizing power. It will become pointless to try to distinguish between music and so-called visual arts because everyone will be a composer, will make images. The universe of technical images can be seen as a universe of musical vision. This essay is an argument in support of this proposition.

Once they have both become electronic, visual and acoustic technologies will no longer be separable. It is almost sad to watch an inherited division between visual and sound arts prevent so-called computer artists from letting their images be audible. This cannot be compared to the resistance film producers showed toward sound film after the First World War, however. At that point, there was still a real technical boundary between image and music, between the world as representation and the world as will. Today this boundary exists only in the thinking of producers working with obsolete categories. On the basis not only of its structure, but also of its technology, so-called computer art is moving toward sounding images and visible sound. And this is the case not only in computer art but in all synthetic images and compositions, even those that present themselves as scientific or political documents rather than as art. Visionary power and music can no longer be separated.

The emerging universe of technical images as both "world as representation" and "world as will"—this formulation of Schopenhauer's—permits very different interpretations, for example, a Nietzschean one: in technical images, the will to power appears in the form of eternal repetition, and in this way, representations become concrete. That is a seductive reading. For the "will to power" can be interpreted as a negatively entropic disposition, and "eternal return of the same" as "reproducibility," and finally, the superman as cybernetic superbrain. I believe, however, that the current tendency to read Nietzsche as a prophet should be taken with a grain of salt, for otherwise, there is a risk of losing one's grasp of what is new in current developments.

I think this new aspect can be grasped at its tip in the dreamlike quality of the emerging image world. It is a dream world in which the dreamers seem exceptionally alert, however, for to press the buttons that produce pictures, the dreamer needs to calculate and compute clear and distinct concepts. It is a dream world, then, that does not lie below waking consciousness but above it, conscious and consciously constructed, a hyperconscious dream world. It will therefore be pointless to try to interpret dreams: they will mean nothing beyond themselves, and they will be tangible—a world of pure art, of play for its own sake. *Ludus imaginis* (play of the image) as *ludus tonalis* (play of sound) and the emerging consciousness of the power to imagine as that of *homo ludens* (man the playful).

What this essay has tried to do is to relate a fable. It narrates a fabulous universe, that of technical images, a fabulous society, that of cybernetic dialogue, a fabulous consciousness, that of making music with the power of imagination. It narrates the story with consummate hope and at the same time with fear and trembling. For this fable is a catastrophe about to break out of its shell. And we are that shell. *De te fabula narratur* (the story is about you).

Summary

These thoughts have followed a twisting path through a thicket of problems. Someone following it may have a feeling of being led about by the nose. It would have been easy to smooth the way, to cut a motorway straight across the thicket of problems, as has been done in the Amazon. But I have some experience with driving, and with the Amazon. Nothing is more boring than a motorway. It is the bends around the problems that make a journey worthwhile. They offer perspectives on the problems.

At the end of this work, an overview is nevertheless appropriate. I will therefore survey the ground that has been covered from a helicopter. Let it be noted, in the meantime, that the Alps are photogenic seen from above, but only by climbing can one experience them.

This essay consists of twenty chapters; that is, twenty problems have been selected from the countless ones that proliferate as the future of technical images approaches. The problems are as follows.

1. *To Abstract:* What are technical images? They differ from all other previous images, and not only because they are made by technical apparatuses (as we mistakenly say). In fact, quite the opposite is true: apparatuses alone may make them because they arise from another level of consciousness, more abstract than that of any previous images.
2. *To Imagine:* From what level of consciousness did earlier pictures arise? From that ancient level at which human beings

first stepped back from their surroundings to observe and to depict, that is to say, from a prehistoric level.

3. *To Make Concrete:* And from what level of consciousness do technical images arise? That level at which we emerge when the world around us and even our own consciousness disintegrates into particles that need to be calculated and composed, which is to say, condensed into images, that is, a visionary level of consciousness.

4. *To Touch:* But these particles are, after all invisible, incomprehensible, and imperceptible. How can we turn them into images? By means of apparatuses equipped with keys, which begs the question of whether and how these keys control the apparatus and how the keys are and should be set up.

5. *To Envision:* If technical images are actually mosaics and not really surfaces, how can we regard them as pictures? By way of the capacity we are currently gaining of seeing something solid in the most abstract things (particles). This does require us to stop trying to tell real from fictional and concern ourselves with the difference between concrete and abstract.

6. *To Signify:* What do technical images, these calculated and computed mosaics, actually mean? They are models that give form to a world and a consciousness that has disintegrated; they are meant to "inform" that world. Their vector of signification is therefore the reverse of that of earlier images: they don't receive their meaning from outside but rather project meaning outward. They lend meaning to the absurd.

7. *To Interact:* How do technical images function as models? They function by means of feedback between themselves and their receivers. People pattern their behavior according to the images, and the images pick up on their behavior to function better and better as models. This feedback is a short circuit that threatens to tip us into entropic decline and to exhaust all history.

8. *To Scatter:* What does a society so fully in the thrall of images

look like? It is a fascistic society, centrally controlled by send-ers, in which traditional social structures have fallen apart and human beings constitute an amorphous, scattered mass. The images contribute to this fragmentation.

9. *To Instruct:* How are the images distributed, to have such power over society? They are produced in automatic apparatuses and passed automatically through channels to their receiv-ers. Within these apparatuses, human beings (functionaries) perform some functions, and nonhuman automata perform others. Functionaries make up the greater part of the society. It is a totalitarianism of the apparatus.

10. *To Discuss:* Is it possible to reorganize the images' fascistic, totalitarian circuitry? Yes, telematics could make it possible. It is a technology of dialogue, and if the images circulated dialogically, totalitarianism would give way to a democratic structure.

11. *To Play:* How can we make images dialogically? Dialogue is an exchange of information that generates new information. It is negatively entropic. Telematics is a game strategy with the goal of steering dialogue toward the production of new information (above all images).

12. *To Create:* Why should anyone participate in such a dialogue, when the result is not his own work but the work of an anony-mous group? People will be drawn in by a desire to play, by the intoxication of creative play.

13. *To Prepare:* So in the future, is anyone potentially a creator? Yes, because telematic dialogue is not only a strategy for producing information but, above all, a school for creativity, a school for freedom.

14. *To Decide:* In such a school, how does one learn to distinguish creativity from imitation, information from redundancy? Tele-matics offers criteria for such critical distinctions and decisions to favor information. It maintains a critical distance.

15. *To Govern:* What would a society in which everyone was creator

and critic look like? It would be a cybernetically controlled net in which the concrete elements would no longer consist of knots (single individuals) but of threads (interpersonal relationships). Along with this dissolution of the "I" into the "we" would come the dissolution of space and time into global simultaneity. It would be a society of simultaneous consensual decisions, a kind of global brain.

16. *To Shrink:* How could such a cerebral society cope with bodily human individuals? It can drain interest from bodies of any sort, including human bodies, redirecting interest instead to immaterial technical images, "pure information." Such a reversal in the vector of interest would result in a strange freedom, namely, contempt for things and conditions.

17. *To Suffer:* But how can we ignore the human body when we live and die with it? The economy and medicine (the struggle against suffering and the delay of death) can be automated and so disappear from view. If suffering cannot be allayed and death becomes desirable, the death must be decided in general dialogue. It would be decided out of sympathy, for when the "I" dissolves in the "we," suffering becomes sympathy.

18. *To Celebrate:* How can anyone so removed from everything physical (all work and all suffering, all activity and passivity), anyone so focused on pure information, live, and would such a life be worthy of the name? This is actually the first life that deserves to be called "human." By comparison to it, all previous forms of life are merely prehuman approximations. Such a life of contemplation of self-made images would be a life of leisure, a celebratory life with others, for others, and in the presence of the absolutely other.

19. *Chamber Music:* What kind of life would such a celebratory one be? It would be like a consciously self-produced dream, a consciously envisioned life; an artificial life in art, life as play with pictures and sounds; a fabulous life that means the whole

essay ends in a fable, albeit one that has now become technically feasible.

20. *Summary:* Can there be an overview of a fable? There can be, but it would render the tale banal and unbelievable. The informative and believable things about it are embedded in the discussion of the nineteen problems listed previously, problems that are current.

Translator's Afterword and Acknowledgments

Nancy Ann Roth

Early in this text, Flusser figures the emerging universe of technical images as a submarine breaking through ice, a powerful ship
shattering a firm, continuous surface into pieces as it rises into
view. Built up over centuries of engagement with alphanumeric
code—with writing—the "ice" that is historical consciousness,
that seems so sturdy, has in fact become vulnerable. The shattering break appears in Flusser's text in verbal images such as the
ship but also more slowly, more subjectively or essayistically, as a
shattering of words. For the figurative ice is made of language, a
structure of sound expanded, honed, solidified through its long
struggle with—or better, against—writing. And the fault lines,
where the ice yields to the force of the rising ship, where particular
signs split and proliferate to carry Flusser's thought, vary from
language to language.

Perhaps the best example is the word *to imagine,* with its rich
resonances in *imagination, imaginary, imaginative,* and *image* itself.
In English, *to imagine* projects a tentative unity amid diversity, an
uneasy truce between an admirable inventiveness and a troubling
tendency to embroider, or misapprehend, reality. It implies but
doesn't necessarily insist on a visually organized expression. Flusser
employs the German verbs *imaginieren, vorstellen,* and *einbilden,*

any of which might justifiably be translated as "to imagine," to describe a new imagination,[1] or perhaps more accurately, to refer to a capacity to communicate visually for which no one word suffices at this point. The rising force of technical images breaks imagining into (at least) two, that is, into a before and an after, into an imagination that can read the world and one that sees it only as illegible whirling particles. Those who can read the world can picture it; those who cannot must envision it, confer a meaning, and rely on apparatuses and keys to do so. Those who "picture" imagine in one way, those who "envision" in quite another. The ice has cracked.

It is just one very modest and yet perhaps sobering example of Flusser's reading of our present situation, his sense of vast change registered in particular words, his sense of such words losing their hold on consciousness, their power to constitute reality, yielding to a very different kind of imagination.

I'd like to extend my warm thanks to Andreas Müller-Pohle, who began to shape this book even before it was written, went on to be its first publisher, and continues to care for it through his support of this English edition. I will not forget Anke Finger's instant enthusiasm when I first told her I wanted to translate Flusser's work into English, and I have been grateful for her steady support ever since. Andreas Ströhl kindly took the time to read and comment most helpfully on an early draft translation, as did Mark Amerika. Lambert Wiesing, a philosopher with a high professional regard and an infectious enthusiasm for Flusser's work, provided most welcome encouragement and timely advice about an English translation. Marcel Marburger generously shared both his knowledge of pertinent materials in the Flusser-Archiv in Berlin and my concern about English equivalents for a few crucial words with unique resonances in German. For all of us, Edith Flusser continues to be an inspiration, a person of enormous warmth and energy, always eager to engage with people and projects that might spark fresh, creative dialogue about her husband's work.

I'd like to thank Doug Armato, Adam Brunner, and Danielle Kasprzak at the University of Minnesota Press for their kindness to me and their commitment to making more of Flusser's work available in English. Finally, it is most fortunate that my husband, Michael Whetman, is an artist who reads voraciously and likes to talk about words. Beyond this, however, he is essential to creating an immediate reality in which I am able to translate books.

Translator's Notes

Warning

1   *Towards a Philosophy of Photography* was first published in 1984 (Göttingen: European Photography); a new translation (London: Reaktion) appeared in 2000.

To Make Concrete

1   William Shakespeare, *The Tempest,* Act IV, scene 1.

To Touch

1   Flusser repeatedly used the Latin phrase *scribere necesse est, vivere non est,* attributed to Heinrich the Sailor (1394–1460), to refer to his own attitude toward writing.

To Signify

1   A phrase from epistemology, proposing that the mind conforms to things or conditions external to it.

To Interact

1   In A.D. 9, Arminius—or Hermann—the leader of a tribe called the Cherusci, living in what is now north Germany, ambushed and defeated three Roman legions led by Quinctilius Varus. Having fought in the Roman army himself, Hermann knew that the legions would be at a disadvantage in the forest terrain with which he and his local tribesmen were familiar. The battle initiated a seven-year war, ultimately establishing the boundary

of the Roman empire at the Rhine rather than the Elbe for the next four hundred years.

To Scatter

1   *Gleichschaltung* was a Nazi neologism meaning "equalization" but referred to the imposition of Nazi policy on broad spectrum of individuals and institutions.

2   Minitel was developed by France Telecom in the early 1980s as a solution to overwhelming new demands for information, especially directory information for the telephone system's many new users. Users were given a small screen and keyboard they could use to access information from a central memory. In Strassbourg, one of the cities where the system was first installed on a trial basis, one programmer adapted the help commands to send and receive messages among users, and suddenly, use of the system rose dramatically. Some of the exchanges were explicitly sexual. Minitel is widely understood to have demonstrated that users were far more keenly interested in the new technology as a means of communicating with one another than with government databases.

To Instruct

1   Democritus was a pre-Socratic philosopher credited with developing the theory of atomism.

To Discuss

1   "Communicology" *(Kommunikologie)* is Flusser's term for the systematic study of communication.

2   A debate between medieval scholastics about the existence of universal qualities, such as wisdom or truth, apart from the manifestation of such qualities in specific objects or individuals.

To Create

1   The Latin phrase meaning "things done" is a legal term, an exception to the rule that hearsay evidence is inadmissible in court.

To Prepare

1   "Even if it is not true, it's a good story."

To Decide

1   Andreas Müller-Pohle, *Transformance* (Göttingen, Germany: European Photography, 1983). Flusser contributed an introduction to this volume.

2   Johann Wolfgang von Goethe, *Faust, Part I, Prologue in Heaven* (1808).

To Shrink

1   "The trumpet casts a wondrous sound," usually associated with Mozart's *Requiem Mass.*

2   T. S. Eliot, *The Hollow Men* (1925).

To Celebrate

1   The realm of the Mothers is something like an underworld, into which Faust descends (*Faust* II, scene 5) and from which he returns, a changed man.

Afterword

1   Vilém Flusser, "A New Imagination," in *Writings,* ed. Andreas Ströhl, trans. Erik Eisel (Minneapolis: University of Minnesota Press, 2002), 110–16.

Index

abstraction: envisioning as
moving from, to concrete, 34,
36–38 (*see also* envisioning);
model of human history as
moving toward higher levels
of, 6–9; need to move back
from, to concrete, 15, 21, 23,
32
actemes, 15
action: as extension of the hand
against the world, 8; images
as models for, 11
adaequatio intellectus ad rem, 46
Anti-Oedipus (Deleuze and
Guattari), xxi
aorist (verb tense in Greek), 129
apparatuses: accelerating
function of, 73; difference
from machine, 24; human
dialogue with, 113;
internal contradiction in
programming of, 18–19;
invention of, 72; loss of
human control over, 73–76;
169, 170, 171; as means of
visualizing the invisible, 16;
"technical" images as those
made by, 7
art: " . . . better than truth,"
(Nietzsche), 139; future

synthesized images as,
103; as imposition of form,
124; music and visual, 165;
technical images as, 124
artificial intelligence:
chimpanzee as, 25; as knot
in information net, 115;
in telematic dialogue with
human intelligence, 113, 161
artists: computer, 165; future
society of 85; venerated as
creative people, 87, 95
author: future disappearance of
the, 99; 111, 123; myth of the,
xvii, 98, 103
authority: rendered superfluous
through copying, 96–97, 123
automatic critics. *See* automata
automata: apparatuses as, 119;
critical consciousness taken
over by, 120–21, 122, 144, 149
automation: as acceleration of
chance events, 73; copying as,
97; danger in, 19; definition
of 19, 73; effect on leisure,
152; revolutionary nature
of, 73

Bacon, Francis, x
Baudrillard, Jean, xi

Vilém Flusser (1920–91) was born in Prague; emigrated to Brazil, where he taught philosophy and wrote a daily newspaper column in São Paulo; and later moved to France. He wrote several books in Portuguese and German. In addition to the University of Minnesota Press's *Writings* volume (2004) and *Does Writing Have a Future?* (Minnesota, 2011), *The Shape of Things, Toward a Philosophy of Photography,* and *The Freedom of the Migrant* have been translated into English.

Mark Poster is professor of history at the University of California, Irvine. His books include *What's the Matter with the Internet?* (Minnesota, 2001), *The Second Media Age, The Mode of Information,* and *Cultural History and Postmodernity.*

Nancy Ann Roth is a writer and critic based in the United Kingdom. She was the translations editor for *German Expressionism: Documents from the End of the Wilhelmine Empire to the Rise of National Socialism,* edited by Rose-Carol Washton Long.